ENGLISH
in Common

1

with ActiveBook

Jonathan Bygrave

Series Consultants
María Victoria Saumell and Sarah Louisa Birchley

ALWAYS LEARNING

PEARSON

ENGLISH in Common 1

with ActiveBook

Maria Victoria Saumell
Sarah Louisa Birchley

PEARSON

English in Common is a six-level course that helps adult and young-adult English learners develop effective communication skills that correspond to the Common European Framework of Reference for Languages (CEFR). Every level of *English in Common* is correlated to a level of the CEFR, and each lesson is formulated around a specific CAN DO objective.

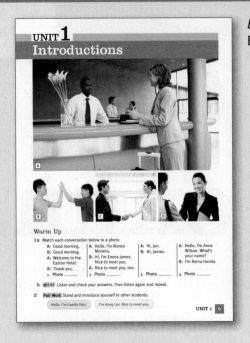

UNIT **1**
Introductions

Warm Up

1a Match each conversation below to a photo.
- A: Good morning.
- B: Good morning.
- A: Welcome to the Easton Hotel.
- B: Thank you.
- 1. Photo ____
- A: Hello. I'm Alonzo Moreno.
- B: Hi. I'm Emma James. Nice to meet you.
- A: Nice to meet you, too.
- 2. Photo ____
- A: Hi, Jun.
- B: Hi, James.
- 3. Photo ____
- A: Hello. I'm Anne Wilson. What's your name?
- B: I'm Reina Honda.
- 4. Photo ____

b ▶1.07 Listen and check your answers. Then listen again and repeat.

2 Pair Work Stand and introduce yourself to other students.

Hello. I'm Camila Díaz.   I'm Hong Lee. Nice to meet you.

UNIT 1   **9**

English in Common 1 has ten units.
Each unit has ten pages.

There are three two-page lessons in each unit.

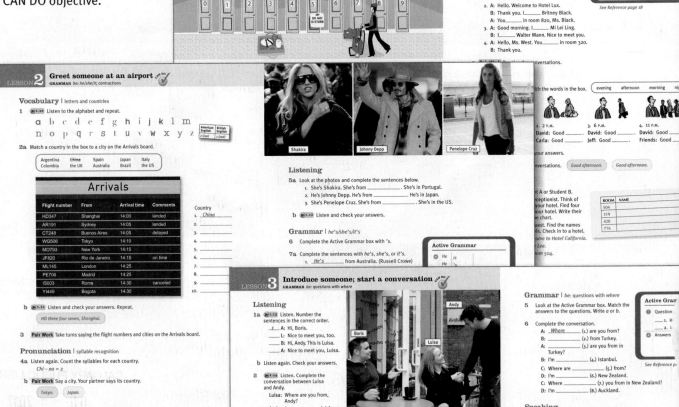

LESSON **1**   **Check in to a hotel**
GRAMMAR be: I/you; contractions

Vocabulary | numbers 0–9
1a ▶1.08 Listen and repeat.

0 1 2 3 4 5 6 7 8 9

DO NOT DISTURB

Grammar | I'm/you're
5a Complete the Active Grammar box with 'm or 're.

b Complete the conversations with 'm or 're.
1. A: Good morning. I'_m_ ____ Mateo Alvarez.
   B: Good morning, Mr. Alvarez. You ____ in room 121.
2. A: Hello. Welcome to Hotel Lux.
   B: Thank you. I ____ Britney Black.
   A: You ____ in room 820, Ms. Black.
3. A: Good morning. I ____ Mi Lei Ling.
   B: I ____ Walter Mann. Nice to meet you.
4. A: Hello, Ms. West. You ____ in room 320.
   B: Thank you.

Active Grammar

+ I	am	Cristina Brand
I		
You	are	in room 329.
You		

See Reference page 18

LESSON **2**   **Greet someone at an airport**
GRAMMAR be: he/she/it; contractions

Vocabulary | letters and countries
1 ▶1.10 Listen to the alphabet and repeat.

a b c d e f g h i j k l m
n o p q r s t u v w x y z

American English z (zee)   British English z (zed)

2a Match a country in the box to a city on the Arrivals board.

Argentina | China | Spain | Japan | Italy
Colombia | the UK | Australia | Brazil | the US

Shakira   Johnny Depp   Penelope Cruz

Arrivals

Flight number	From	Arrival time	Comments
HD347	Shanghai	14:00	landed
AR191	Sydney	14:05	landed
CT248	Buenos Aires	14:05	delayed
WG606	Tokyo	14:10	
MO793	New York	14:15	
JF820	Rio de Janeiro	14:15	on time
ML145	London	14:25	
PE706	Madrid	14:25	
IS003	Rome	14:30	canceled
YI449	Bogota	14:30	

Country
1. _China_
2. ____
3. ____
4. ____
5. ____
6. ____
7. ____
8. ____
9. ____
10. ____

b ▶1.11 Listen and check your answers. Repeat.

HD three four seven, Shanghai.

3 Pair Work Take turns saying the flight numbers and cities on the Arrivals board.

Pronunciation | syllable recognition
4a Listen again. Count the syllables for each country.

Chi – na = 2

b Pair Work Say a city. Your partner says its country.

Tokyo.   Japan.

Listening

5a Look at the photos and complete the sentences below.
1. She's Shakira. She's from ____. She's in Portugal.
2. He's Johnny Depp. He's from ____. He's in Japan.
3. She's Penelope Cruz. She's from ____. She's in the US.

b ▶1.12 Listen and check your answers.

Grammar | he's/she's/it's
6 Complete the Active Grammar box with 's.

7a Complete the sentences with he's, she's, or it's.
1. _He's_ ____ from Australia. (Russell Crowe)

Active Grammar

He	is
He	

evening   afternoon   morning   nig...

2. 2 P.M.   3. 6 P.M.   4. 11 P.M.
David: Good ____   David: Good ____   David: Good ____
Carla: Good ____   Jeff: Good ____   Friends: Good ...

...your answers.

...conversations.   Good afternoon.   Good afternoon.

...t A or Student B.
...ceptionist. Think of
...your hotel. Find four
...our hotel. Write their
...e chart.
...uest. Find the names
...is. Check in to a hotel.
...ome to Hotel California.
... Lee.
...oom 504.

ROOM	NAME
504	
319	
428	
716	

LESSON **3**   **Introduce someone; start a conversation**
GRAMMAR be: questions with where

Listening

1a ▶1.13 Listen. Number the sentences in the correct order.
- _1_ A: Hi, Boris.
- ___ L: Nice to meet you, too.
- ___ B: Hi, Andy. This is Luisa.
- ___ A: Nice to meet you.

Boris   Luisa   Andy

b Listen again. Check your answers.

2 ▶1.14 Listen. Complete the conversation between Luisa and Andy.
- Luisa: Where are you from, Andy?
- Andy: I ____ (1.) from the US.
- Luisa: Where ____ (2.) you from in the US?
- Andy: I'm from New York. Where are ____ (3.) from?
- Luisa: I'm ____ (4.) Argentina.
- Andy: Where are you from in Argentina?
- Luisa: I'm from Rosario.

Pronunciation | sentence stress
3a ▶1.15 Listen. Mark the stress.
1. Where are you from?
2. Where are you from in the US?
3. I'm from New York.

Rosario, Argentina   New York, USA

Grammar | be: questions with where
5 Look at the Active Grammar box. Match the answers to the questions. Write a or b.

6 Complete the conversation.
- A: _Where_ ____ (1.) are you from?
- B: ____ (2.) from Turkey.
- A: ____ (3.) are you from in Turkey?
- B: I'm ____ (4.) Istanbul.
- C: Where are ____ (5.) from?
- D: I'm ____ (6.) New Zealand.
- C: Where ____ (7.) you from in New Zealand?
- D: I'm ____ (8.) Auckland.

Active Gram...

Question	
	1. ...
	2. ...
Answers	

See Reference p...

Speaking

7 Group Work Work in groups of three: A, B, and C. Use your own c... or your own ideas.
- Student A: Introduce B and C.
- Student B: Ask where Student C is from.
- Student C: Ask where Student B is from.

Vocabulary | common phrases
8a Match the phrases in the box to the conversations.

No, thank you.   Yes, please.   Pardon?   Excuse me ...

1   2   3

A two-page Unit Wrap Up and a Reference page end each unit.

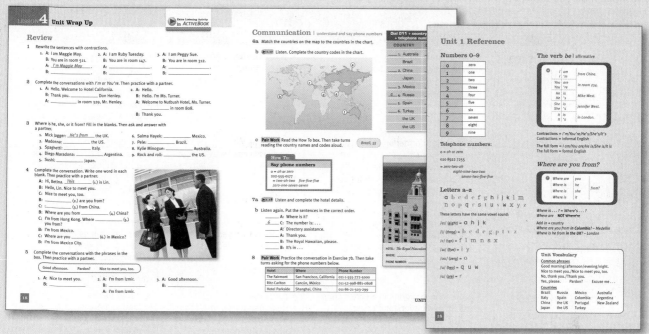

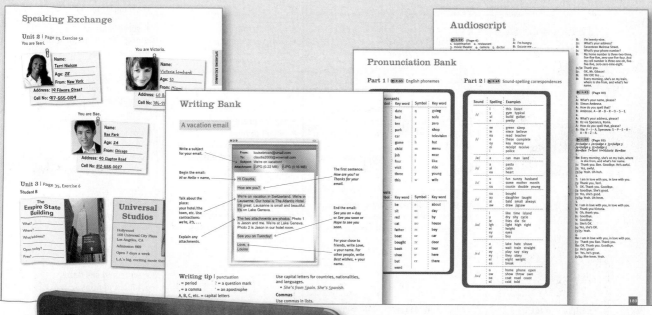

Back of Student Book

- Each Student Book contains an **ActiveBook**, which provides the Student Book in digital format. *ActiveBook* also includes the complete Audio Program and Extra Listening activities.

- An optional online **MyEnglishLab** provides the opportunity for extra practice anytime, anywhere.

- The Teacher's Resource Book contains teaching notes, photocopiable extension activities, and an **ActiveTeach**, which provides a digital Student Book enhanced by interactive whiteboard software. *ActiveTeach* also includes the videos and video activities, as well as the complete Test Bank.

Contents

UNIT	CAN DO OBJECTIVES	GRAMMAR	VOCABULARY/EXPRESSIONS
1 Introductions page 9	• check in to a hotel • greet someone at an airport • introduce someone • start a conversation	• *be: I/you/he/she/it* • contractions • *be*: questions with *where*	• numbers 0–9 • greetings • letters and countries • common phrases • saying room numbers/names • greeting someone at an airport
2 Family and friends page 19	• give basic information about your family • ask for and give personal details • give information about other people • write a short personal profile	• questions with *who/what* • possessive adjectives: *my/your/his/her* • articles: *a/an*	• numbers 10–99 • descriptive adjectives: opinions • occupations • talking about age • asking for spelling • saying email addresses
3 Traveling page 29	• write a simple vacation email • say what's in your suitcase • ask about tourist attractions	• *be: we/they*; contractions • *be*: negative; *yes/no* questions • possessive adjectives: *our/their* • plural nouns	• descriptive adjectives: places • vacation things • days of the week • using *here* and *there*
4 Stores and restaurants page 39	• order food and drink in a coffee shop • ask for and understand prices • ask about things and make simple transactions	• *can*: requests • demonstratives: *this/that/these/those* • possessive nouns: *'s*	• public places • food and drink • clothes and colors • talking about prices • irregular plurals • buying tickets • asking where something is
5 Things to see and do page 49	• give a simple description of a place • ask about a new town • ask where important places are • talk about general abilities	• *there is/there are* • *can/can't*: ability	• *some/a lot of* • prepositions of location • nationalities • skills • telling time • giving an opinion • greeting a friend
6 All about you page 59	• say what you like/don't like • have a conversation with someone you don't know • talk about the routines of people you know	• simple present • object pronouns • *wh-* questions: *who/what/where* and short answers	• descriptive adjectives: people • jobs and activities • daily activities • saying you don't understand • showing interest
7 A day at work page 69	• understand simple instructions • say how often you do something • welcome a visitor to your place of work	• imperatives • adverbs of frequency • *would like*: preferences and offers	• places of work • more jobs • simple requests • months • job duties • ordinal numbers • write and say dates • food and drink
8 Your likes and dislikes page 79	• explain why you want to do something • say what things you possess • suggest a restaurant • make reservations • order food	• *can*: possibility • *like* + gerund/infinitive • *want* + infinitive • *have/has* • *wh-* question words: *which/how*	• leisure activities • rooms and furniture • food • making suggestions • reserving a table at a restaurant
9 Your life page 89	• make simple statements about people from history • give a short description of a past experience • make a simple request and ask permission	• simple past of *be* • *can/could I*: permission • *can/could you*: requests	• collocations with prepositions • time expressions: *yesterday, last, ago* • housework • talking about childhood • discussing an experience
10 Past and future events page 99	• understand a simple narrative of past events • give a simple summary of a news event • talk about immediate and long-term plans	• simple past: regular and irregular verbs • *be going to*	• verbs: life events • future plans • saying large numbers

READING/WRITING	LISTENING	COMMUNICATION/ PRONUNCIATION
Reading texts: • an airport arrivals board • an ad for vacations • hotel contact information **Writing task:** conversation completion	**Listening tasks:** • identify situations • place in sequence • identify room numbers and phone numbers • determine nationalities	**Communication:** understand and say phone numbers **Pronunciation:** • alphabet • syllable recognition • sentence stress
Reading texts: • an efriends profile • a family tree **Writing task:** a brief personal profile	**Listening tasks:** • determine relationships • perceive personal details • correct addresses • identify occupations	**Communication:** talk about favorite people and things **Pronunciation:** word stress in numbers
Reading texts: • an email about a New York vacation • advertisements for tourist attractions **Writing task:** a simple vacation email	**Listening tasks:** • discern details • identify subject pronouns • recognize the main ideas	**Communication:** have an extended phone conversation **Pronunciation:** plural "*s*"
Reading texts: • menus • information about a shopping district • an email **Writing task:** a paragraph about a shopping area	**Listening tasks:** • recognize the main idea • identify details • determine prices • identify situations • detect specific words	**Communication:** ask for and give locations **Pronunciation:** linking
Reading texts: • a short article about Washington D.C. • a map • a class schedule • job ads **Writing task:** a paragraph about a favorite place to visit	**Listening tasks:** • understand directions • identify the gist • distinguish abilities • recognize key information	**Communication:** check in to a bed and breakfast **Pronunciation:** vowel clarity in *can* and *can't*
Reading texts: • personal profiles • brief essays about friends and family • an email • a web questionnaire and key **Writing task:** a paragraph about a friend/family member	**Listening tasks:** • understand the gist • identify likes and dislikes • identify people • distinguish between true and false information	**Communication:** ask and answer questions about a friend **Pronunciation:** *yes/no* questions: intonation
Reading texts: • an article about a teacher's typical day • a questionnaire • a short handwritten note • a calendar **Writing task:** a note making a request	**Listening tasks:** • identify situations • recognize key phrases • recognize key information • understand location	**Communication:** get and give directions in a building **Pronunciation:** word stress
Reading texts: • a technology quiz • a scoring key • a restaurant menu **Writing task:** an email to a hotel	**Listening tasks:** • understand the gist • identify places • recognize key words	**Communication:** ask for and give information about people **Pronunciation:** reduction of sounds: *want to*
Reading texts: • biographies of famous people • an article about househusbands **Writing task:** a paragraph about your first teacher	**Listening tasks:** • understand the gist • identify key words • recognize situations	**Communication:** talk about school days **Pronunciation:** sentence stress
Reading texts: • a three-part article about a famous painting • short articles about good and bad news • a list of sales prices **Writing task:** a journal entry about a good/bad week	**Listening tasks:** • distinguish between true and false information • determine prices • understand main ideas	**Communication:** talk about past and future vacations **Pronunciation:** simple past *-ed* endings

How much do you know . . . ?

International words

1 ▶ 1.02 Do you know these words? Match each word in the box to its picture. Write the words. Then listen and check.

bus	pizza	soccer	restaurant	~~supermarket~~
taxi	tennis	camera	doctor	television
hotel	police	phone	university	movie theater

1. _supermarket_

3. _movie_

4. _camera_

5. _doctor_

8. _hotel_

9. _pizza_

7. _bus_

11. _taxi_

13. _____

12. _____

14. _____

2. _____

6. _____Soccer_____

10. _____tennis_____

15. _____

Numbers and alphabet

2 ▶ 1.03 Do you know these numbers? Listen and repeat.

0	1	2	3	4
zero	one	two	three	four
5	6	7	8	9
five	six	seven	eight	nine

3 ▶ 1.04 Do you know the English alphabet? Listen and repeat.

a	b	c	d	e
A	B	C	D	E
f	g	h	i	j
F	G	H	I	J
k	l	m	n	o
K	L	M	N	O
p	q	r	s	t
P	Q	R	S	T
u	v	w	x	y
U	V	W	X	Y
z				
Z				

Useful language

4a Do you know classroom instructions? Match each instruction in the box to its picture below. Write each word on the line.

> ~~Listen~~   Look   Read   Write   Speak   Repeat   Match

1.

Listen

2.

_____

3.

_____

4.

_____

5.

_____

6.

_____

7.

_____

b ▶ 1.05 Listen and check your answers.

5 ▶ 1.06 Learn these useful phrases. Listen and repeat. How do you say them in your language? Write them below.

English	Translation
Sorry, I don't understand.	_____
What's *"Hola"* in English?	_____
Can you say that slowly, please?	_____
Excuse me, can you help me?	_____

UNIT 1
Introductions

Warm Up

1a Match each conversation below to a photo.

A: Good morning.	A: Hello. I'm Alonzo Moreno.	A: Hi, Jun.	A: Hello. I'm Anne Wilson. What's your name?
B: Good morning.		B: Hi, James.	
A: Welcome to the Easton Hotel.	B: Hi. I'm Emma James. Nice to meet you.		B: I'm Reina Honda.
B: Thank you.	A: Nice to meet you, too.		
1. Photo _____	2. Photo _____	3. Photo _____	4. Photo _____

b ▶1.07 Listen and check your answers. Then listen again and repeat.

2 **Pair Work** Stand and introduce yourself to other students.

> Hello. I'm Camila Diaz.

> I'm Hong Lee. Nice to meet you.

Vocabulary | numbers 0–9

1a ▶1.08 Listen and repeat.

b Write the numbers next to the words.

_____ four	_____ eight	_____ one	_____ two	_____ five
_____ seven	_____ six	_____ three	_____ zero	_____ nine

2 Point to a number. Your partner says the number. Change roles after nine numbers.

3a Read the How To box. Write the room numbers.

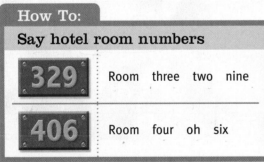

How To:

Say hotel room numbers

329	Room three two nine
406	Room four oh six

1. 129   Room *one two nine*

2. 438   Room _____ _____ _____

3. 517   Room _____ _____ _____

4. 209   Room _____ _____ _____

5. 608   Room _____ _____ _____

6. 345   Room _____ _____ _____

b Say the room numbers.

4 **Pair Work** Read the How To box below. Then practice the conversation with your names. Change roles and partners several times.

How To:

Say names

Mr. Smith	Mrs./Ms./Miss Jones

A: *Hello.*

B: *Hi. I'm Leonardo Gallo.*

A: *Welcome to Bally Hotel, Mr. Gallo. You're in room 502.*

B: *Thank you.*

Grammar | *I'm/you're*

5a Complete the Active Grammar box with *'m* or *'re*.

b Complete the conversations with *'m* or *'re*.

1. **A:** Good morning. I*'m* Mateo Alvarez.
   B: Good morning, Mr. Alvarez. You _are_ in room 121.

2. **A:** Hello. Welcome to Hotel Lux.
   B: Thank you. I _are_ Britney Black.
   A: You_____ in room 820, Ms. Black.

3. **A:** Good morning. I_____ Mi Lei Ling.
   B: I_____ Walter Mann. Nice to meet you.

4. **A:** Hello, Ms. West. You_____ in room 320.
   B: Thank you.

c **Pair Work** Practice the conversations.

Active Grammar

⊕ I	am	
I	_am_	Cristina Branco.
You	are	
You	_are_	in room 329.

See Reference page 18

Vocabulary | greetings

6a Complete the sentences with the words in the box.

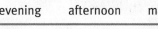
evening   afternoon   morning   night

1. 8 A.M.
   David: Good _____.
   Betty: Good _____.

2. 2 P.M.
   David: Good _____.
   Carla: Good _____.

3. 6 P.M.
   David: Good _even_.
   Jeff: Good _____.

4. 11 P.M.
   David: Good _____.
   Friends: Good _____.

b ▶ 1.09 Listen and check your answers.

c **Pair Work** Practice the conversations.   (Good afternoon.)   (Good afternoon.)

Speaking

7 **Pair Work** Choose Student A or Student B.

Student A: You are a receptionist. Think of a name for your hotel. Find four guests for your hotel. Write their names in the chart.

Student B: You are a guest. Find the names of four hotels. Check in to a hotel.

A: *Good evening. Welcome to Hotel California.*
B: *Thank you. I'm Chin Lee.*
A: *Mr. Lee. You're in room 504.*
B: *Thank you.*

ROOM	NAME
504	
319	
428	
716	

Vocabulary | letters and countries

1 ▶1.10 Listen to the alphabet and repeat.

a b c d e f g h i j k l m
n o p q r s t u v w x y z

American English	British English
z (zee)	z (zed)

2a Match a country in the box to a city on the Arrivals board.

> Argentina   ~~China~~   Spain   Japan   Italy
> Colombia   the UK   Australia   Brazil   the US

Arrivals

Flight number	From	Arrival time	Comments
HD347	Shanghai	14:00	landed
AR191	Sydney	14:05	landed
CT248	Buenos Aires	14:05	delayed
WG506	Tokyo	14:10	
MO793	New York	14:15	
JF820	Rio de Janeiro	14:15	on time
ML145	London	14:25	
PE706	Madrid	14:25	
IS003	Rome	14:30	canceled
YI449	Bogota	14:30	

Country
1. *China*
2. _____
3. _____
4. *Japan*
5. *The U.S*
6. *Brazil*
7. *U.K*
8. *Spain*
9. *Italy*
10. *Colombia*

b ▶1.11 Listen and check your answers. Repeat.

> HD three four seven, Shanghai.

3 Pair Work Take turns saying the flight numbers and cities on the Arrivals board.

Pronunciation | syllable recognition

4a Listen again. Count the syllables for each country.

Chi – na = 2

b Pair Work Say a city. Your partner says its country.

> Tokyo.   Japan.

Shakira

Johnny Depp

Penelope Cruz

Listening

5a Look at the photos and complete the sentences below.

1. She's Shakira. She's from _____. She's in Portugal.
2. He's Johnny Depp. He's from _____. He's in Japan.
3. She's Penelope Cruz. She's from _____. She's in the US.

b ▶1.12 Listen and check your answers.

Grammar | *he's/she's/it's*

6 Complete the Active Grammar box with *'s*.

7a Complete the sentences with *he's*, *she's*, or *it's*.

1. *He's* _____ from Australia. (Russell Crowe)
2. _____ from the US. (Angelina Jolie)
3. _____ in Japan. (Osaka)
4. _____ from Spain. (Antonio Banderas)
5. _____ in China. (Beijing)
6. _____ from Australia. (Nicole Kidman)
7. _____ from Mexico. (Gael García Bernal)
8. _____ from Argentina. (The tango)

> ### Active Grammar
>
> | ➕ | He | is | |
> |---|-----|------|------------------|
> | | He | 's | |
> | | She | is | *from Japan.* |
> | | She | _____ | *from Argentina.* |
> | | It | is | |
> | | It | _____ | |
>
> *See Reference page 18*

b **Pair Work** Make true or false statements about cities and people.

> Sydney is in Argentina.   False! It's in Australia.

> Tom Cruise is from the US.   True.

Speaking

8 **Pair Work** Read the How To box. Then practice greeting your partner at the arrivals gate at the airport.

> **How To:**
> **Greet someone at airport arrivals**
> A: *Mr. Depp?*
> B: *Yes.*
> A: *Hello, Mr. Depp. I'm Yuki Suzuki. Welcome to Japan.*
> B: *Thank you.*

Listening

1a ▶1.13 Listen. Number the sentences in the correct order.

   _1_ **A:** Hi, Boris.

   _____ **L:** Nice to meet you, too.

   _____ **B:** Hi, Andy. This is Luisa.

   _____ **A:** Nice to meet you, Luisa.

b Listen again. Check your answers.

2 ▶1.14 Listen. Complete the conversation between Luisa and Andy.

Luisa: Where are you from, Andy?

Andy: I _____ (1.) from the US.

Luisa: Where _____ (2.) you from in the US?

Andy: I'm from New York. Where are _____ (3.) from?

Luisa: I'm _____ (4.) Argentina.

Andy: Where are you from in Argentina?

Luisa: I'm from Rosario.

Boris | Luisa | Andy

Pronunciation | sentence stress

3a ▶1.15 Listen. Mark the stress.

1. <u>Where</u> are you <u>from</u>?
2. Where are you from in the US?
3. I'm from New York.

b Listen again. Repeat.

Rosario, Argentina

New York, USA

Speaking

4a **Group Work** Work in groups of three. Repeat the conversation in Exercise 2.

b **Group Work** Read the How To box, then close your books. Introduce each other.

How To:

Introduce people

This is (Paul).
Nice to meet you.
Nice to meet you, too.

Hi, Britta. | Hi, Carlos. This is Roxana.

Grammar | *be*: questions with *where*

5 Look at the Active Grammar box. Match the answers to the questions. Write *a* or *b*.

6 Complete the conversation.

A: _Where_ (1.) are you from?

B: _____ (2.) from Turkey.

A: _____ (3.) are you from in Turkey?

B: I'm _____ (4.) Istanbul.

C: Where are _____ (5.) from?

D: I'm _____ (6.) New Zealand.

C: Where _____ (7.) you from in New Zealand?

D: I'm _____ (8.) Auckland.

Active Grammar

? Questions

____	**1.** Where are	you	from?
____	**2.** Where are	you	from in the US?

+ Answers

	a. I	'm	from Las Vegas.
	b. I	'm	from the US.

See Reference page 18

Speaking

7 **Group Work** Work in groups of three: A, B, and C. Use your own country or city, or your own ideas.

Student A: Introduce B and C.

Student B: Ask where Student C is from.

Student C: Ask where Student B is from.

Vocabulary | common phrases

8a Match the phrases in the box to the conversations.

> No, thank you.   ~~Yes, please.~~   Pardon?   Excuse me . . .

A: Coffee?
B: _Yes, please._

A: Black pepper?
B: _____

A: I'm hungry.
B: _____

A: He's Ronaldinho from Brazil.
B: _____

b ▶1.16 Listen and check your answers.

c **Pair Work** Practice the conversations with a partner.

Review

1 Rewrite the sentences with contractions.

1. **A:** I am Maggie May.
   B: You are in room 511.
   A: _I'm Maggie May_ .
   B: _____ .

2. **A:** I am Ruby Tuesday.
   B: You are in room 147.
   A: _____ .
   B: _____ .

3. **A:** I am Peggy Sue.
   B: You are in room 312.
   A: _____ .
   B: _____ .

2 Complete the conversations with *I'm* or *You're*. Then practice with a partner.

1. **A:** Hello. Welcome to Hotel California.
   B: Thank you. _____ Don Henley.
   A: _____ in room 329, Mr. Henley.

2. **A:** Hello.
   B: Hello. I'm Ms. Turner.
   A: Welcome to Nutbush Hotel, Ms. Turner. _____ in room 808.
   B: Thank you.

3 Where is he, she, or it from? Fill in the blanks. Then ask and answer with a partner.

1. Mick Jagger: _He's from_ the UK.
2. Madonna: _____ the US.
3. Spaghetti: _____ Italy.
4. Diego Maradona: _____ Argentina.
5. Sushi: _____ Japan.
6. Salma Hayek: _____ Mexico.
7. Pele: _____ Brazil.
8. Kylie Minogue: _____ Australia.
9. Rock and roll: _____ the US.

4 Complete the conversation. Write one word in each blank. Then practice with a partner.

A: Hi, Betina. _This_ (1.) is Lin.
B: Hello, Lin. Nice to meet you.
C: Nice to meet you, too.
B: _____ (2.) are you from?
C: _____ (3.) from China.
B: Where are you from _____ (4.) China?
C: I'm from Hong Kong. Where _____ (5.) you from?
B: I'm from Mexico.
C: Where are you _____ (6.) in Mexico?
B: I'm from Mexico City.

5 Complete the conversations with the phrases in the box. Then practice with a partner.

> Good afternoon.   Pardon?   Nice to meet you, too.

1. **A:** Nice to meet you.
   B: _____

2. **A:** I'm from Izmir.
   B: _____
   A: I'm from Izmir.

3. **A:** Good afternoon.
   B: _____

Communication | understand and say phone numbers

Dial 011 + country code + telephone number	
COUNTRY	**CODE**
____ 1. Australia	____
Brazil	55
____ 2. China	*87*
Japan	81
____ 3. Mexico	*52*
a 4. Russia	____
____ 5. Spain	____
____ 6. Turkey	____
the UK	44
the US	1

6a Match the countries on the map to the countries in the chart.

b ▶1.17 Listen. Complete the country codes in the chart.

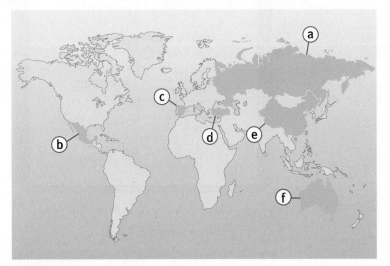

c **Pair Work** Read the How To box. Then take turns reading the country names and codes aloud.

Brazil, 55

> ### How To:
> **Say phone numbers**
>
> o = *oh* or *zero*
> 202-555-0177
>   = *two-oh-two   five-five-five*
>   *zero-one-seven-seven*

7a ▶1.18 Listen and complete the hotel details.

b Listen again. Put the sentences in the correct order.

_____ A: Where is it?
__6__ C: The number is: . . .
_____ A: Directory assistance.
_____ A: Thank you.
_____ B: The Royal Hawaiian, please.
_____ B: It's in . . .

8 **Pair Work** Practice the conversation in Exercise 7b. Then take turns asking for the phone numbers below.

Hotel	Where	Phone Number
The Fairmont	San Francisco, California	011-1-555-772-5000
Ritz-Carlton	Cancún, México	011-52-998-881-0808
Hotel Parkside	Shanghai, China	011-86-21-503-299

HOTEL: *The Royal Hawaiian*
WHERE: _____, *Hawaii.*
PHONE NUMBER: _____

Unit 1 Reference

Numbers 0–9

0	zero
1	one
2	two
3	three
4	four
5	five
6	six
7	seven
8	eight
9	nine

Telephone numbers:

0 = *oh* or *zero*

020 8922 7255

= *zero-two-oh*
    eight-nine-two-two
        seven-two-five-five

Letters a–z

a b c d e f g h i j k l m
n o p q r s t u v w x y z

These letters have the same vowel sound:

/eɪ/ (eight) = a h j k

/i/ (three) = b c d e g p t v z

/ɛ/ (ten) = f l m n s x

/aɪ/ (five) = i y

/oʊ/ (zero) = o

/u/ (two) = q u w

/ɑ/ (are) = r

The verb *be* | affirmative

Contractions = *I'm/You're/He's/She's/It's*
Contractions = informal English

The full form = *I am/You are/He is/She is/It is*
The full form = formal English

Where are you from?

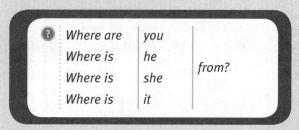

Where is . . . ? = *Where's . . . ?*
Where are   **NOT** ~~Where're~~

Add *in* + country
*Where are you from **in Colombia**? – Medellin*
*Where is he from **in the UK**? – London*

Unit Vocabulary

Common phrases
Good morning/afternoon/evening/night.
Nice to meet you./Nice to meet you, too.
No, thank you./Thank you.
Yes, please.   Pardon?   Excuse me . . .

Countries

Brazil	Russia	México	Australia
Italy	Spain	Colombia	Argentina
China	the UK	Portugal	New Zealand
Japan	the US	Turkey	

UNIT 2
Family and friends

Warm Up

1 Look at photo A above. Fill in the blanks below with the words from the box.

> mother   husband   sister   daughter   father   son   wife   brother

1. Karen — Luke = _mother_ — _son_
2. John — Lucy = _____ — _____
3. Lucy — Luke = _____ — _____
4. John — Luke = _____ — _____
5. Karen — John = _____ — _____
6. Karen — Lucy = _____ — _____

2a Match the objects 1–9 in photos B–D with the words in the box.

> _1_ phone number   ___ email address   ___ address   ___ cell phone   ___ map
> ___ laptop   ___ passport   ___ first name   ___ last name

b ▶1.19 Listen and check your answers. Repeat.

Tom, ____

Anna, ____

Marek, ____

Sofia, ____

Sabrina, 32

James, ____

Sarah, ____

Carl, ____

Listening

1a Look at the photos. Write the ages next to the names in the photos.

26	32	3	38
1	57	60	22

b ▶1.20 Listen and check your answers.

c Listen again. Write a name next to each word below.

mother = _____   brother = _____   son = _____   daughter = _____

father = _____   sister = _____   wife = *Sabrina*   husband = _____

Vocabulary | numbers 10–99

2 ▶1.21 Listen and repeat. Then close your books. Say the numbers.

10 ten	**12** twelve	**14** fourteen	**16** sixteen	**18** eighteen
11 eleven	**13** thirteen	**15** fifteen	**17** seventeen	**19** nineteen

3a ▶1.22 Listen and repeat.

20 twenty	**40** forty	**60** sixty	**80** eighty	**21** twenty-one
30 thirty	**50** fifty	**70** seventy	**90** ninety	**99** ninety-nine

b **Pair Work** Write a number. Your partner says it. | 27 | (*twenty-seven*)

Grammar | *Who . . . ?; my*

4 Complete the Active Grammar box with *he* and *she*.

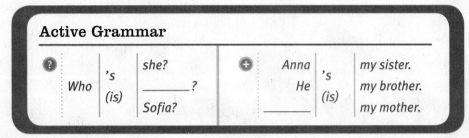

Active Grammar

?	Who	's (is)	she? _____ ? Sofia?	⊕	Anna He	's (is)	my sister. my brother. my mother.
					_____		

See Reference page 28

5 Complete these sentences for Sabrina.

1. Carl is _my brother_ .
2. Anna is _____ .
3. Marek is _____ .
4. Sofia is _____ .
5. Tom is _____ .
6. James is _____ .

6 **Pair Work** Complete the dialogs. Then practice with a partner.

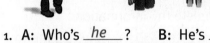

1. **A:** Who's _he_ ? **B:** He's _____ father.
2. **A:** _____ she? **B:** _____ my mother.

3. **A:** Who's _____? **B:** _____ _____ brother.
4. **A:** _____ he? **B:** It's OK. _____ _____ friend.

Pronunciation | word stress in numbers

7 ▶1.23 Listen. Circle the correct number. Then listen again and repeat.

1. He's my brother. He's (13)/ 30 years old.
2. Carol's my sister. She's 14/ 40 years old.
3. She's Helen. She's 18/ 80 years old.
4. My son's 15/ 50 years old.
5. He's my husband. He's 16/ 60 years old.

Speaking

8a Read the How To box. Then write five names from your family or friends.

b **Pair Work** Explain to your partner who the people are.

Who's Martin?   He's my brother. He's 27 years old.

How To:		
Talk about age		
How old is he/she?		
He's	62	years old.
She's	21	

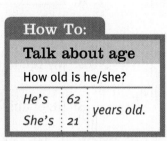

Ask for and give personal details

CAN DO ✓

GRAMMAR questions with *what*; possessive adjective: *your*

Listening

1a ▶1.24 The young man in the photo is Ben. Listen and complete the information.

a. Name: Ben _____

b. From: _____

c. Age: _____ years old

d. Address: _____ Melrose Street

e. Home phone number: _____

f. Cell phone number: _____

b Listen again and check your answers.

Grammar | *What's your . . . ?*

2 Complete the questions in the Active Grammar box with words from the box.

> number   your   name   phone

3a Write questions from the Active Grammar box for these answers.

1. A: *What's your phone number?*

   B: My home number is 212-555-0124.

2. A: _____

   B: 81 East Avenue, New York.

3. A: _____

   B: My cell number is 917-555-0038.

4. A: _____

   B: Stephanie Brown.

Active Grammar

❓

		your _____ ?
What	**'s** (is)	_____ address?
		your _____ number?
		your cell phone _____ ?

See Reference page 28

American English	British English
cell phone	mobile phone

b **Pair Work** Ask and answer the questions in the Active Grammar box.

Speaking

4a Read the How To box.

b ▶1.25 Listen and write the correct names and addresses.

1. Simon _____

2. 82 _____ _____ , Rome

5a Your teacher will assign you one person below. Go to page 109 in the Speaking Exchange and complete the chart for your person.

How To:

Ask for spelling

A: *What's your name?*

B: *John Carax.*

A: *How do you spell that?*

B: *C – A – R – A –X.*

	Name	Age	From	Address	Phone Number

b **Group Work** Roleplay. Talk to other students and complete the chart.

> *Hello. What's your name?*   *I'm Bae.*   *How do you spell that?*

Vocabulary | expressions

6a Match an expression (*great*, *good*, *OK*, *bad*, *awful*) to each judge.

b ▶1.26 Listen to the auditions. What do the judges say about each singer? Complete column 1 in the chart below.

c **Pair Work** What do you think of the singers? Complete column 2 and compare with a partner.

> *Ben's awful.*   *Yes, he's awful. Terri's OK.*

d **Pair Work** Talk about other singers you know.

1. ____ 2. ____ 3. ____ 4. *Great.* 5. ____

	1. Judges	2. You
Ben	*He's awful.*	
Terri	She is gre	
Victoria		
Bae		

Reading

1a Look at the profiles. Which person is from Canada? from Japan? from Germany?

http://www.emailfriends.net

e-mail Friends

Email address _____   Sign in
Password _____

REGISTER HERE!

Friends Search

ENTER FIRST NAME HERE

ENTER LAST NAME HERE

SEARCH _____

- School friends
- College friends
- Childhood friends
- Work friends
- Team friends
- Neighbors

RESULTS

a. I'm Frieda Lang. I'm from Munich. I'm 52 years old. I'm a _____ .
frieda@teachernet.de

b. Hello. My name's Tom Mackintosh. I'm 34 years old. I'm an _____ . I'm from Toronto.
tom@mackintosh.com

c. My name's Junko Nakamura. I'm from Kyoto. I'm 18. I'm a _____ .
junura@jmail.jp

Listening

b ▶1.27 Listen and fill in the blanks in the profiles with an occupation from the box.

> accountant   teacher   student

2a Read the How To box. Say the email addresses in the profiles.

b **Pair Work** Exchange email addresses with several other students.

> A: *What's your email address?*
> B: *It's henrique99@vista.com*
> A: *How do you spell that?*
> B: *Henrique: H – E – N . . .*

How To:

Say email addresses

john.smith@email.com

"john dot smith at email dot com"

Vocabulary | occupations

3 ▶1.28 Match the pictures to the occupations in the box. Then listen and check.

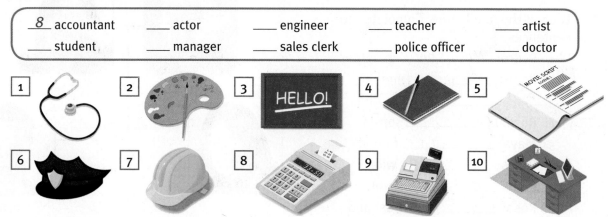

_8_ accountant		___ actor		___ engineer		___ teacher		___ artist	
___ student		___ manager		___ sales clerk		___ police officer		___ doctor	

1	2	3 HELLO!	4	5 MOVIE SCRIPT
6	7	8	9	10

Grammar | a/an and his/her

4 Complete the Active Grammar box with *a* or *an*.

5a Put the words from Exercise 3 in the correct column.

a	an

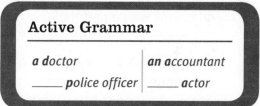

> **Active Grammar**
>
> | *a doctor* | *an accountant* |
> |---|---|
> | ___ *police officer* | ___ *actor* |
>
> *See Reference page 28*

b **Pair Work** Talk about your family members' occupations.

6 Complete the Active Grammar box with *his, he's, her,* or *she's*.

> **Active Grammar**
>
> **?** *What's his name?*   *What's her name?*
> _____ *name's Tom.*   _____ *name's Maria.*
> *What's* _____ *occupation?*   *What's* _____ *occupation?*
> _____ *an accountant.*   _____ *a student.*

See Reference page 28

Speaking

7 **Pair Work** Ask a partner about his or her best friend. Talk to several partners.

(*Who's your best friend?*)   (*Her name's Nina.*)   (*What's her occupation?*)

Writing

8a Write a personal profile for emailfriends.net.

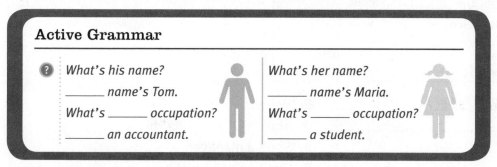

My name's . . . I'm from . . .
I'm . . . years old and I'm a . . . .

b **Group Work** Exchange information with a partner. Then tell your group about your partner.

Review

1 Look at the family tree. Complete the sentences.

Pedro   Rosa

Maya   Raúl

1. Pedro: _Maya's my_ daughter
2. Raúl: _____ mother.
3. Maya: _____ brother.
4. Rosa: _____ son.
5. Maya: _____ father.
6. Pedro: _____ wife.
7. Raúl: _____ sister.
8. Rosa: _____ husband.

2 Use the words to write questions. Then take turns asking and answering the questions with a partner.

1. address/your/What's
   What's your address _____?

2. phone/What's/number/your
   _____?

3. name/your/What's
   _____?

4. are/How/you/old
   _____?

5. you/Where/from/are
   _____?

6. spell/How/that/you/do
   _____?

3 Write the questions. Then take turns asking and answering them with a partner.

Ms. Letterman	Mr. Kuroda
First name: Helen	First name: Takao
Age: 33	Age: 42
Job: manager	Job: police officer
From: Australia	From: Japan

1. A: _What's her first name?_ _____ B: Helen.
2. A: _____ B: She's 33.
3. A: _____ B: She's a manager.
4. A: _____ B: She's from Australia.
5. A: _____ B: Takao.
6. A: _____ B: He's 42.
7. A: _____ B: He's a police officer.
8. A: _____ B: He's from Japan.

4 Circle the correct word.

1. six + six = _eleven/(twelve)/thirteen_
2. She's a _doctor/actor/great_.
3. What's your _passport/phone/address_?
4. He's an _teacher/accountant/student_.
5. Who's your favorite _singer/restaurant/city_?
6. What's your _email/phone number/ computer number_?

Communication | talk about favorite people and things

5a Match the words in the box to the pictures.

> __3__ actor _____ singer _____ CD _____ city _____ movie _____ book _____ restaurant

b **Pair Work** Take turns asking about the pictures.

> *What's number 2?*   *It's a restaurant.*

6a **Group Work** Ask three classmates about their favorite things. Use the box on the left to make questions. Write their answers in the chart on the right.

		restaurant? actor? CD?
What's Who's	your favorite	city? singer? movie? book?

	Name:	Name:	Name:
city			
restaurant			
singer			
movie			
book			
CD			
actor			

> *Who's your favorite singer?*   *Beyoncé. She's great.*   *Beyoncé? She's OK.*

b **Pair Work** Tell a new partner about your three classmates.

> *Juan's favorite city is Rio de Janeiro. His favorite restaurant is . . .*

Unit 2 Reference

Questions

Who is for people.

> **Who** is he?
> **Who** is Rachel?
> **Who**'s your best friend?

What is for things.

> **What**'s her last name?
> **What**'s his phone number?
> **What**'s your email address?

Who's . . . ? and *What's . . . ?* = informal English

Who's she?

She's my manager.

Who is . . . ? and *What is . . . ?* = formal written English

Remember these questions with **How** . . . ?

> **How** do you spell that?
> **How** old are you?
> **How** old is he/she?

Possessive adjectives: *my/your/his/her/its*

My, your, his, her, and *its* are possessive adjectives. Possessive adjectives show ownership.

Pronoun	Possessive adjective
I am Robert.	**My** name is Robert.
You are 32.	**Your** sister is 21.
He is a singer.	Paul is **his** brother.
She is great.	**Her** CD is great.
It is a movie.	Avatar is **its** name.

Articles: *a/an*

Use *a* and *an* before singular nouns.

> She's **a** teacher.
> Her brother is **an** actor.

a + consonant sound

> **a** car, **a** phone, **a** website

an + vowel sound

> **an** email address, **an** actor, **an** engineer

Numbers 10–99

10	11	12	13	14
ten	eleven	twelve	thirteen	fourteen
15	**16**	**17**	**18**	**19**
fifteen	sixteen	seventeen	eighteen	nineteen

20	twenty	21	twenty-one
30	thirty	37	thirty-seven
40	forty	44	forty-four
50	fifty	58	fifty-eight
60	sixty	65	sixty-five
70	seventy	76	seventy-six
80	eighty	82	eighty-two
90	ninety	99	ninety-nine

Unit Vocabulary

Family

mother	sister	wife	husband
father	brother	son	daughter

Personal details

first name	phone number
last name	email address
address	cell phone number

Adjectives

great	good	OK	bad	awful

Jobs

accountant	actor	manager
sales clerk	artist	engineer
police officer	doctor	teacher

UNIT 3
Traveling

Warm Up

1a Match each photo to a word in the box.

> _____ a beach _____ a pyramid _____ a palace _____ a museum

b ▶1.29 Listen to the words in the box and repeat. Then check the meanings in a dictionary.

> a river   a department store   a theme park   a mountain   a lake

2 Complete these famous tourist attractions with the words above.

1. The Yellow _River_ in China
2. The Hermitage _____ in Moscow
3. Buckingham _____ in London
4. The Great _____ of Giza in Egypt
5. Macy's _____ in New York
6. Sugar Loaf _____ in Rio de Janeiro
7. _____ Titicaca in Bolivia
8. Universal Studios _____ in California

Disney Concert Hall, Los Angeles

South Beach, Miami

The French Quarter, New Orleans

Central Park, New York

Vocabulary | adjectives

1 Look at the photos of US tourist attractions. Then circle the correct adjective in each sentence.

  1. The Disney Concert Hall in Los Angeles is *modern/old*.

  2. The French Quarter in New Orleans is *beautiful/ugly*.

  3. South Beach in Miami is *boring/exciting*.

  4. Central Park in New York City is *big/small*.

2 **Pair Work** Talk about three tourist attractions in your country.

> The Forbidden City in Beijing is beautiful.

Reading

3a María and Estéban are on a tour of the US. Read the email. Who are their new friends?

b Mark each statement true (*T*) or false (*F*).

  _____ 1. María and Estéban are in New York City.

  _____ 2. María and Estéban's room is old.

  _____ 3. Hiro and Yoko are from Japan.

  _____ 4. Hiro and Yoko's English is awful.

  _____ 5. New York is boring.

c Underline all the adjectives in the email.

From: maria55@gmail.com
To: jane.clark@yahoo.co.uk
Subject: We're in New York!

Hi Jane,

Estéban and I are in New York City now. **We're** at the W Hotel. It's in Times Square. **Our** room is very modern. The views are great.

Hiro and Yoko are our new friends. **They're** on the tour, too. They're from Japan. They're nice and **their** English is good.

New York is exciting!

Love, María

Grammar 1 | *be with* we *and* they

4 Use the email on page 30 to complete the Active Grammar box.

5 Complete the sentences. Use contractions.

1. They _'re_ from Sydney.
2. You _____ from Spain.
3. We _____ in Buenos Aires.
4. It _____ modern.
5. She _____ my daughter.
6. I _____ in the photo.
7. They _____ in the department store.
8. He _____ great.

Active Grammar

⊕	I	'm (am)	41.
	You	're (are)	my friend.
	He		my father.
	She	's (is)	my mother.
	It		a museum.
	You	're (are)	my friends.
	We	_____ (_____)	in Rome.
	They	_____ (_____)	from Peru.

See Reference page 38

Grammar 2 | our *and* their

6 Complete the Active Grammar box below.

Active Grammar

I	She is **my** friend.	It	**Its** beach is nice.
You	**Your** house is modern.	You	**Your** photos are beautiful.
He	Rachel is **his** wife.	We	Andrea is _____ friend.
She	**Her** mother is great.	They	_____ daughter is in the park.

See Reference page 38

7 Circle the correct word.

1. Are they *we're*/(*our*) books?
2. *We're*/*Our* in Kyoto.
3. *They're*/*Their* photos are great.
4. *They're*/*Their* from Mexico.
5. Where is *we're*/*our* hotel?
6. *They're*/*Their* in the photo.

Writing

8a **Pair Work** You and your partner are on vacation. Choose a destination from the photos on page 30. Complete the details.

1. My partner is _____. (name)
2. We are in _____. (place) It is _____. (adjective)
3. Our friends are _____ and _____. (names)
4. Our hotel is _____. (name) Our room is _____. (adjective)

b Look at the Writing Bank on page 116. Then write an email to a friend about your vacation.

Say what's in your suitcase

GRAMMAR plural nouns; the negative of *be*

Vocabulary | vacation things

American English	British English
pants	trousers

1a Match each picture to a word or phrase in the box.

> <u>2</u> camera   ___ book   ___ skirt   ___ sweater   ___ suitcase   ___ pair of pants
>
> ___ T-shirt   ___ map   ___ blouse   ___ MP3 player   ___ backpack   ___ pair of shoes

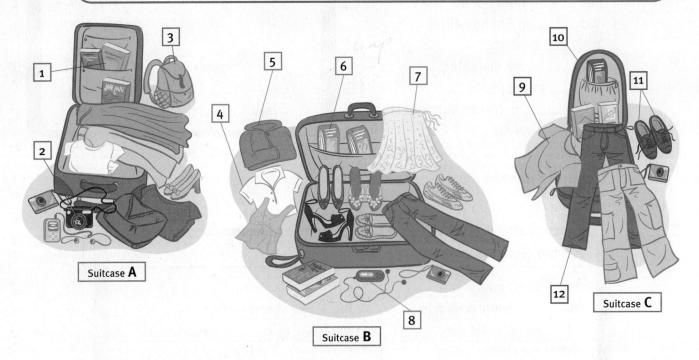

Suitcase **A**

Suitcase **B**

Suitcase **C**

b ▶1.30 Listen and check your answers. Mark the stress and repeat.   *a su̱itcase*

Listening

2 ▶1.31 Listen. Match each conversation to a suitcase in the pictures above.

1. suitcase ____   2. suitcase ____   3. suitcase ____

Grammar | plural nouns

3 ▶1.32 Listen again to Conversation 3 above. Complete the Active Grammar box.

> ### Active Grammar
>
> | one book | _____ book**s** |
> |---|---|
> | a blouse | _____ blouse**s** |
> | one pair of shoes | five pair**s** of _____ |
>
> See Reference page 38

Pronunciation | plural "*s*"

4a ▶1.33 Listen. How is the "*s*" pronounced: /s/, /z/, or /ɪz/?

___ a. two suitcase<u>s</u>   ___ d. three camera<u>s</u>   ___ g. eight sweater<u>s</u>

___ b. five map<u>s</u>   ___ e. two pair<u>s</u> of shoes   ___ h. six skirt<u>s</u>

___ c. seven blouse<u>s</u>   ___ f. four book<u>s</u>

b Listen again and check your answers. Then repeat.

Speaking

5a **Pair Work** Describe a suitcase from Exercise 1a on page 32. Your partner guesses the suitcase.

> What's in the suitcase?

> Two skirts, a pair of shoes, three books . . .

b **Pair Work** Cover one of the suitcases. Remember what's in it. Tell your partner.

c **Pair Work** What is in your suitcase when you go on vacation? Tell your partner.

Listening

6a  Listen. Answer the questions.

  1. What is her name? 2. What is in her suitcase?

b Listen again. Complete the phrases from the conversation.

  Jane: _____'m not Miss Smith. **Jane:** _____ isn't a camera. **Jane:** _____ aren't books.

Grammar | the negative of *be*

7 Look at Exercise 6b. Then complete the Active Grammar box with *aren't* or *isn't*.

8 Circle the correct answer.

  1. You *'m not*/*aren't* an actor.
  2. I *'re not*/*'m not* from Brazil.
  3. She *aren't*/*isn't* my sister.
  4. It *isn't*/*'m not* my camera.
  5. We *aren't*/*isn't* in room 232.
  6. He *'m not*/*isn't* my brother.

Active Grammar

I	'm not (am not)	Miss Smith.
You	aren't (are not)	in room 324. 21.
He She	_____ (is not)	my brother. my sister.
It	_____ (is not)	a camera.
We	_____ (are not)	from the US. students.
They	_____ (are not)	friends. in Korea.

See Reference page 38

Speaking

9a **Pair Work** Use the chart to make statements. Write ✓ or ✗.

	From this city	A good singer	Under 21 years old	A manager	In Canada
You	✗				
Your partner					

> I'm from this city.

> I'm not from this city. I'm from Acapulco.

b Write sentences using the chart in Exercise 9a.

> I'm from this city. Carlos isn't from this city. He's from Acapulco. We're good singers.

Vocabulary | days of the week

1a ▶1·35 Listen and repeat the days of the week.

| Monday | Tuesday | Wednesday | Thursday | Friday | Saturday | Sunday |

b **Pair Work** Say a day. Your partner says the next day. *Thursday.* *Friday.*

Reading

2a Look at the ads. What tourist attraction is each ad for?

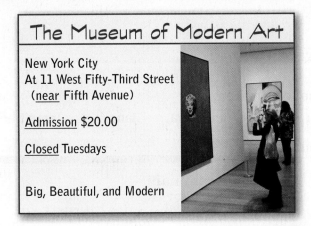

The Museum of Modern Art

New York City
At 11 West Fifty-Third Street
 (near Fifth Avenue)

Admission $20.00

Closed Tuesdays

Big, Beautiful, and Modern

The Smithsonian
National Air and Space Museum

Washington, D.C.
On Independence
 Avenue at Sixth Street

Admission free

Open 7 days a week

b Look at the underlined words in the text. Check the meanings in a dictionary.

c Read the ads. Circle the correct word in the sentences below.
1. The Museum of Modern Art *is/isn't* closed on Mondays.
2. The Museum of Modern Art *is/isn't* in New York City.
3. The Smithsonian National Air and Space Museum *is/isn't* free.
4. The Smithsonian National Air and Space Museum *is/isn't* open seven days a week.
5. The Museum of Modern Art *is/isn't* free.
6. The Smithsonian National Air and Space Museum *is/isn't* in New York.

Listening

3a ▶1·36 Listen. Which tourist attraction are the hotel clerk and guest talking about?

b Read the How To box. Then listen again and complete the phrases below with *here*, *there*, and *Here's*.
1. Is it near ___here___?
2. It's about 6 blocks from _____ . _____
 a map. We're _____, and it's _____ .

> **How To:**
>
> **Use *here* and *there***
>
> *It's here.*
>
> *It's there.*
>
> *Here's a map.*

Grammar | *be: yes/no* questions

4a Compare the ➕ and ❓ forms below:

  ➕ The museum *is* in New York.

  ❓ *Is* the museum in New York?

b Complete the Active Grammar box with *Is, Are,* or *Am*.

5 Use the words to write questions. Then write short answers.

1. open/Is/today/it

  A: <u>Is it open today</u> ?

  B: <u>Yes, it is</u> .

2. you/Korea/Are/from

  A: _____?

  B: No, _____.

3. the US/Is/from/she

  A: _____?

  B: Yes, _____.

4. a museum/it/Is

  A: _____?

  B: No, _____.

5. Is/open/the store

  A: _____?

  B: Yes, _____.

6. you/an actor/Are

  A: _____?

  B: No, _____.

Active Grammar

❓

Am	I	your friend?	Yes, you are. / No, you aren't.
_____	you	from Italy?	Yes, I am. / No, I'm not.
_____	he / she / it	your brother? / your sister? / open?	Yes, he/she/it is. / No, he/she/it isn't.
_____	we	near the lake?	Yes, we are. / No, we aren't.
_____	they	in London?	Yes, they are. / No, they aren't.

See Reference page 38

Reading

6 **SPEAKING EXCHANGE** Ask and answer questions about tourist attractions.

Student A: Read the ad below about the Empire State Building and answer your partner's questions. Ask for information about Universal Studios.

Student B: Look at page 109. Read the ad about Universal Studios and answer your partner's questions. Ask for information about the Empire State Building.

> What is it?

> It's a big building with beautiful views.

The Empire State Building

A BIG building with beautiful views!

Fifth Avenue at 34th Street New York City

Admission $20

Open 7 days a week

Universal Studios

What? _____

_____

Where? _____

_____

What/address? _____

Open 7 days a week? _____

Free? _____

Review

1 Read the information in the box.
Complete the paragraph with
we're, our, they're, or *their.*

	Susana and I	Ken and Keiko
From?	Argentina	Japan
Job?	doctors	teachers
House?	in Buenos Aires	in Osaka
Where now?	on vacation in Hawaii	on vacation in France

Ken and Keiko are _our_____ (1.) friends. _____ (2.) from Japan and
_____ (3.) teachers. Susana and I are from Argentina. _____ (4.) doctors.
_____ (5.) house is in Buenos Aires. _____ (6.) house is in Osaka. Right
now, _____ (7.) on vacation in France. _____ (8.) on vacation in Hawaii.

2 Complete the negative sentences with a word from the box.

> aren't   not   isn't   'm   You   I   She

1. I_'m_____ not a student. I'm a
   teacher.
2. It _____ open today. It's open
   tomorrow.
3. You _____ a good singer.
4. _____ isn't from Canada.
5. You _____ 21. You're 23.

6. _____'m not from Brazil.
7. You _____ my friend.
8. She _____ my sister. She's my
   mom.
9. _____ aren't in room 324. You're
   in room 325.
10. I'm _____ Peter. I'm Tom.

3 Use the words to write questions.

1. near/palace/the/we/Are
   _Are we near the palace_____ ?
2. museum/Is/open/the
   _____ ?
3. Australia/they/from/Are
   _____ ?
4. she/your/Is/friend
   _____ ?

5. here/the/near/lake/Is
   _____ ?
6. department stores/Are/today/open/the
   _____ ?
7. we/Are/City Hotel/in/the
   _____ ?
8. suitcase/your/Is/this
   _____ ?

4 **Pair Work** Write short answers for each question in Exercise 3. Then take turns
asking and answering with a partner.

1. (✓) _Yes, we are_____ .
2. (✗) _No, it isn' t_____ .
3. (✓) _____ .
4. (✗) _____ .

5. (✓) _____ .
6. (✗) _____ .
7. (✓) _____ .
8. (✗) _____ .

Communication | have an extended phone conversation

5a Put the words in the box in the correct columns.

skirt	small	suitcase	book	food	old	bad	beautiful
ugly	hot	cold	backpack	good	nice	camera	modern
big	map	awful	great	new	exciting	boring	

Nouns	Adjectives
skirt	*small*

b Which words follow *very*: nouns or adjectives?

6 ▶ **1·37** Listen and read the conversation. Answer the questions below.

Louis: Hello.

Sara: Hi, Louis. It's Sara.

Louis: Hi, Sara. How are you and Paul?

Sara: We're fine, thanks. And you?

Louis: Fine, thanks. Where are you?

Sara: We're in France.

Louis: Are you in Provence?

Sara: No, we aren't. We're in Paris.

Louis: Is it beautiful?

Sara: Yes, it is. It's very beautiful.

Louis: Is it cold?

Sara: No, it isn't. It's not very cold.

Louis: Is your hotel nice?

Sara: No, it isn't. It's very small and very old.

Louis: Too bad! Is the food good?

Sara: Yes, it's very, very good. Are Mom and Dad OK?

Louis: Yes, they are. They're fine.

Sara: OK, see you on Friday.

Louis: See you on Friday. Bye.

Sara: Bye.

Hot   Very hot

1. Where are Sara and Paul?
2. Are they in Provence?
3. Is Paris beautiful?
4. Is Paris hot?
5. Is the hotel nice?
6. Is the food good?

7a **Pair Work** Practice the conversation. Change roles.

b **Pair Work** Practice making new conversations. Use new people, new places, and other adjectives from Exercise 5b.

> Hello.   Hi, Carmen. It's Flavio.   Hi, Flavio. How are you and your wife?

Reference

to be

I	'm (am)	
You	're (are)	
He		
She	's (is)	in California.
It		from Colombia.
We	're (are)	
They	're (are)	

⊖			
I	'm not (am not)	Miss Smith.
You	aren't (are not)	in room 324.
		21 years old.
He		my brother.
She	isn't (is not)	my sister.
It		a camera.
We	aren't (are not)	from the US.
		students.
They	aren't (are not)	friends.
		in Korea.

?			Short answers
Am	I	your friend?	Yes, you are. / No, you aren't.
Are	you	from Italy?	Yes, I am. / No, I'm not.
Is	he / she / it	your brother? / your sister? / open?	Yes, he/she/it is. / No, he/she/it isn't.
Are	we	near the lake?	Yes, we are. / No, we aren't.
Are	they	in London?	Yes, they are. / No, they aren't.

Also possible:

He's/She's/It's not
We're/You're/They're not
   They're not at home.

Possessive adjectives

Pronoun	Possessive adjective
I'm from New York.	My wife is from Rome.
You're in Tokyo.	Your son is in London.
He's my brother.	His name is Jeff.
She's my sister.	Her daughter is three.
It's not a big hotel.	Its name is "W."
We're on vacation.	Our hotel is very nice.
They're in Italy.	Their children are at home.

Days of the week

weekdays: Monday, Tuesday, Wednesday, Thursday, Friday

the weekend: Saturday, Sunday

Use *on* + days of the week
   Her birthday is **on** Monday.

Adjectives

old	cold	small	boring
big	nice	good	closed
hot	new	great	modern
bad	ugly	awful	exciting
free	OK	open	beautiful

Noun + *be* + adjective
   It's modern.   They're great.

Noun + *be* (+*a/an*) + adjective + noun
   She's a good teacher.   It's a big market.

Unit Vocabulary

Tourist attractions

a river	a pyramid	a museum
a lake	a palace	a theme park
a beach	a building	a mountain
a bridge	a department store	

Vacation things

map	sweater	backpack
skirt	camera	MP3 player
book	suitcase	pair of pants
shirt	blouse	pair of shoes

Stores and restaurants

Warm Up

1a Match each place in the box to a photo above or a small picture below.

____ ATM	____ drugstore	____ supermarket	____ train station
____ bank	____ bookstore	____ newsstand	____ movie theater
____ bus stop	____ restaurant	____ parking lot	____ outdoor market

American English	British English
ATM	cash point
drugstore	chemist

b ▶1.38 Listen and check your answers. Then repeat.

2 **Pair Work** Ask *What's your favorite . . . ?*

> *What's your favorite supermarket?*

> *Grand Foods is my favorite.*

Vocabulary | food and drink

1a Label the food and drink in each photo with a phrase from the box below.

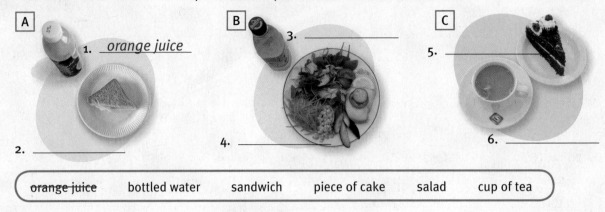

A	B	C
1. *orange juice*	3. _____	5. _____
2. _____	4. _____	6. _____

orange juice	bottled water	sandwich	piece of cake	salad	cup of tea

b ▶1.39 Listen. Match a photo above to each conversation.

_____ Conversation 1   _____ Conversation 2   _____ Conversation 3

2a Listen to the three conversations in Exercise 1b again. Complete the phrases below with the words in the box.

chocolate	large	house	ham and cheese	small

1. a _house_ salad
2. a _____ bottled water
3. a _____ sandwich
4. a _____ orange juice
5. a piece of _____ cake

b Check your answers in Audioscript 1.39 on page 124.

Grammar | *can:* requests

3 Look at the Active Grammar box. Match a phrase on the left to a phrase on the right.

4a Complete the conversations with the words or phrases in the Active Grammar box.

    A: Hello. Can I help you?

    B: Yes. _____ (1.) iced tea, please?

    A: Certainly. Anything _____ (2.)?

    B: Yes, please. _____ (3.) small house salad, too?

    A: Sure.

    C: _____ (4.) large coffee, please?

    A: Certainly. _____ (5.) else?

    C: No, _____ (6.).

> ### Active Grammar
>
> | 1. *Can I have a* | *orange juices, please?* |
> |---|---|
> | 2. *Can I have an* | *chicken sandwich, please?* |
> | 3. *Can I have two* | *iced tea, please?* |
>
> *Certainly/Sure. Anything else?*
>
> *No, that's all./Yes, please. Can I have . . . ?*
>
> *See Reference page 48*

b **Pair Work** Practice the conversation in pairs. Change roles.

Pronunciation | linking

5 ▶1.40 Listen and repeat.

Can I . . . ? /kæ – naɪ/

Can I have a . . . ? /kæ – naɪ – hæ – və/

Can I have a small coffee?

/kæ – naɪ – hæ – və – smɔl – kɑ fi/

Vocabulary | prices in English-speaking countries

6a Complete the chart.

$1.50	one	(dollar and)	fifty	(cents)
€2.99	two	(euros and)	_____	(cents)
£5.25	five	(pounds and)	_____	(pence)

b ▶1.41 Listen. Circle the correct price.

1. a. $1.00   b. $1.10   c. $1.20
2. a. $2.98   b. $3.89   c. $3.98
3. a. $8.19   b. $8.90   c. $8.99
4. a. €15.17   b. €15.18   c. €15.70
5. a. €4.34   b. €3.34   c. €4.43
6. a. £3.13   b. £3.19   c. £3.39

Countries using $ include:
Australia, Belize, Canada, Jamaica, New Zealand, Singapore, and the US.

c **Pair Work** Say a price. Your partner writes the price.

Speaking

7 **Pair Work** Read the How To box. Look at the menu.

Student A: You are a server in a coffee shop.

Student B: You are a customer. Order food and drink.

Drinks	small	medium	large
Tea	$1.45	$1.75	$1.85
Coffee	$1.60	$1.90	$2.00
Espresso	$1.55	$1.85	$2.15
Iced Tea	$1.60	$1.85	$1.95
Bottled water	$ .95	$1.25	$1.50
Orange juice	$3.00	$3.60	$4.10
Food			
House salad		$4.45	
House salad with chicken		$5.95	
Chicken salad sandwich		$6.35	
Roast beef sandwich		$6.90	
Ham and cheese sandwich		$6.75	

How To:

Order food and drink

A: *Can I help you?*

B: *Can I have a salad, please?*

A: *Sure. Anything else?*

B: *No, that's all./*
Yes, can I have a coffee, too?

A: *For here or to take out/to go?*

B: *For here./To take out./To go.*

A: *That's $6.05.*

Ask for and understand prices

CAN DO ✓

GRAMMAR demonstratives: *this / that / these / those*

Reading

1a Match each question to its correct answer.

- _1_ What is it?
- ___ Is it big?
- ___ Where is it?
- ___ What is for sale there?
- ___ What stores are there?

b Pair Work Ask and answer the questions.

2 Pair Work What's your favorite shopping area or store? Ask and answer the questions from Exercise 1a.

Rodeo Drive

1. Rodeo Drive is a very famous shopping street.
2. It's in Beverly Hills, California.
3. It's about three blocks long.
4. Designer clothes and jewelry are for sale on Rodeo Drive.
5. Prada, Chanel, Tiffany, and many other stores are there.

Vocabulary | clothes and colors

3a Look at the pictures. Match the colors to the clothes.

a green T-shirt

1. green — a. pair of shoes
2. white — b. skirt
3. orange — c. coat
4. red — d. pair of pants
5. yellow — e. blouse
6. black — f. dress
7. blue — g. bag
8. brown — h. hat
9. pink — i. T-shirt

b ▶1·42 Listen and check your answers.

c Pair Work What clothes and colors are in your classroom?

A blue-and-white shirt.

Listening

4a ▶1·43 Listen. Write the prices in the picture.

b Listen again. Complete the questions with *this, that, these,* or *those*.

1. How much is _____ blue hat?
2. How much are _____ beautiful dresses?
3. How much is _____ yellow skirt?
4. How much are _____ white shirts?

Grammar | *this/that/these/those*

5 Complete the Active Grammar box with *that, these,* or *those*.

$ _____

$ _____

$ _____

that /those

this/these

$ _____

$ _____

Active Grammar

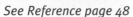

this	hat
_____	bag
_____	bracelets
_____	sweaters

See Reference page 48

Speaking

6 **Pair Work** Read the How To box. Take turns asking and answering about the prices in Exercise 4a.

Writing

7 Write a paragraph about your favorite shopping area. Use the article about Rodeo Drive to help you.

> My favorite shopping area is . . . It's in . . .

Stefan

A

Mike

Kyra

B

Jack
WILL CALL

C

Vocabulary | irregular plurals

1a Match a description below to each photo.

_____ 1. a man, a woman, and a child at a train station

_____ 2. a man and a woman buying tickets at a theater

_____ 3. people in a supermarket

b Complete the chart of irregular plurals.

Singular	Plural
one person	two _people_
one _____	two men
one woman	two _____
one _____	two children

Listening

2a ▶1.44 Listen. Match each conversation to a photo in Exercise 1a.

_____ Conversation 1   _____ Conversation 2   _____ Conversation 3

b Listen again. Fill in the blanks in the conversations.

1. **A:** Can I have three _tickets_ (1.) to Boston, please? Two adults and one child.

   B: One-way or round-trip?

   A: Round-trip, please.

   B: That's forty-two thirty, please. Thank you. _____ (2.) you are.

2. **A:** Can I _____ (3.) two tickets for *Legally Blonde*, please?

    B: That's ninety-eight ninety, please.

    A: _____ (4.) I pay by credit card?

    B: Sure. Sign here, please. Thank you. Here you are.

    A: Thanks.

3. **A:** Your groceries come to thirty-one dollars and seven cents.

    B: Here _____ (5.) are. It's a debit card.

    A: Enter your PIN _____, (6.) please. Thank you.

3   **Pair Work** Practice the conversations.

4   **Pair Work** Read the How To box. Close your books. Create new conversations in a store or train station.

How To:

Pay for things

A: *Can I have three tickets to Boston, please?*   **A:** *Can I pay by credit card?*

B: *One-way or round-trip?*   **B:** *Yes. Sign here, please. Here you are.*

A: *One way.*   **A:** *It's a debit card.*

B: *That's $42.30.*   **B:** *Enter your PIN number, please.*

Grammar | possessive nouns: *'s*

5a Match the things below to people in the photos on page 44.

1. _Jack_   2. _____ 3. _____

Active Grammar

Use *'s* to show possession.

1. *They're Jack**'s** theater tickets.*

2. *She's* _____ *daughter.*

3. *It's* _____ *train ticket.*

See Reference page 48

b Complete the sentences about Jack, Mike, and Stefan in the Active Grammar box.

6   Rewrite the sentences with the name + *'s*.

1. It's his passport. (Kevin)
    It's Kevin's passport.

2. They're her shoes. (Rosie)
    _____

3. This is his email address. (Takumi)
    _____

4. What is her cell number? (Adele)
    _____

Speaking

7a Each student gives something to the teacher (**Ex:** a bag, a pencil).

b Guess who each thing belongs to.   *Is that Anna's bag?*   *No, it isn't. It's Helen's bag.*

Review

1 Complete the sentences with *Can I have* + *a*, *an*, or *two*.

1. _Can I have an_ espresso, please?
2. _____ iced tea, please?
3. _____ house salad, please?
4. _____ pieces of cake, please?

2 Number these sentences in the correct order to make a conversation. Then practice with a partner.

_____ That's $4.55, please.

_____ Yes. Can I have a chicken salad sandwich and an espresso, please?

_____ Take out.

_____ No, that's all.

_1_ Good morning. Can I help you?

_____ To eat here or take out?

_____ Certainly. Anything else?

3 Circle the correct word in each sentence. Then practice with a partner.

1. **A:** What's *this/that/these/those* near your bed?
   B: It's my new sweater.

2. **A:** How much are *this/that/these/those* shirts here?
   B: They're $12.99 each.

3. **A:** Here you are.
   B: What's *this/that/these/those*?
   A: It's a present. Happy birthday!

4. **A:** What are *this/that/these/those* sandwiches on that table?
   B: They're roast beef.

4 Rewrite the sentences with possessive *'s*.

1. He is Jamie. This is his suitcase.
   This _is Jamie's suitcase_ .

2. She's Dorota. That's her baby.
   That's _____ .

3. He's Placido. They're his daughters.
   They're _____ .

4. That's Jay. That is his restaurant.
   That's _____ .

5 Correct the possessive *'s* in this email. There are four mistakes.

> From: jay@totalmail.com
> To: pat@englishmail.com
> Subject: my wife*'s* parents!
>
> Hi Pat
>
> How are you? Our house is very busy. Ann's mother, Hilda, is here. She's in Paul bedroom. Paul is in Tom bedroom with Tom. They aren't happy. Bob, Hilda husband, isn't here. He's at home with Hilda dog!
>
> See you soon,
> Jay

6 Unscramble the <u>underlined</u> letters to make words.

1. What's your favorite *tsrtuaenar*?   r_estaurant_ _____

2. Excuse me, where is the *artni antsiot*?   t_____ s_____

3. How much is a *dbetotl rawet*?   b_____ w_____

4. That *genoar* skirt is nice.   o_____

5. Is that Sharon's *clbak gba*?   b_____ b_____

Communication | ask for and give locations

7a Match each sentence below to a picture. Write A, B, C, or D.

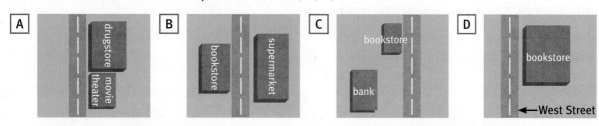

____ 1. It's on West Street.

____ 2. It's across from the bookstore.

____ 3. It's next to the movie theater.

____ 4. It's near the bank.

b ▶1.45 Listen and complete the map with places in the box.

> cell phone store   train station   supermarket

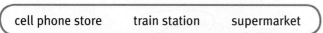
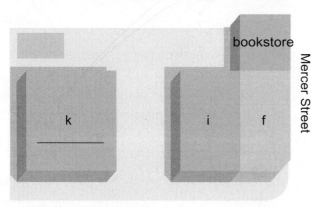
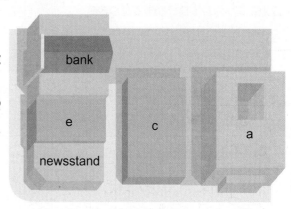
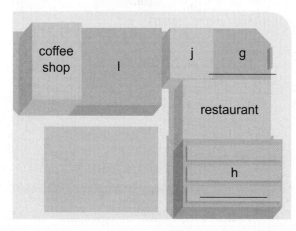
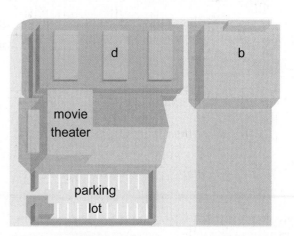

8a **Pair Work** Look at the How To box. Ask questions about the map using the building and street names.

b **SPEAKING EXCHANGE** Ask questions about your map. Your partner gives you the information.

Student A: Look at page 112.

Student B: Look at page 110.

> **How To:**
>
> **Ask where something is**
>
> A: *Excuse me, where's the . . . ?*
> B: *It's . . . / I'm sorry. I don't know.*
> A: *Thank you.*
> B: *You're welcome.*

Unit 4 Reference

can: requests

Can I have	a piece of cake, an espresso, an orange juice, a ticket to Paris, two bottled waters,	please?
Certainly/Sure.		

Use *Can I have . . . ?* to ask for things in stores/coffee shops/train stations, etc.

this/that/these/those

this

these

that

those

	near	far
Singular	*this*	*that*
Plural	*these*	*those*

How much are **those** shirts?
Are **these** books free?
That hat is great!
This sweater is beautiful.

Possessive nouns: *'s*

Use *'s* to show possession.

Mary is Dylan**'s** daughter.
Those are Jody**'s** tickets.

Be careful not to confuse possessive *'s* (as in *Jody's tickets*) with contraction *It's = It is*. Possessive: *its*

Irregular noun plurals

Regular plurals = noun + s

ticket → ticket**s**

Other plurals:
Words ending in -s, -sh, -ch → add -es /ɪz/

sandwich—sandwich**es**   address—address**es**

Words ending in -y → change y to i and add -es

baby—bab**ies**

Words ending in -ife → change f to v

wife—wi**ves**

Some nouns are irregular in the plural.

child → children   woman → women
man → men   person → people

Prices

To ask and answer about prices, use:

How much is/are . . . ?	It's/They're . . .
How much is that computer?	It's $799.
How much are those books?	They're $8.

When you say prices, it is normal to leave out the currency.

$12.20   twelve twenty   €1.99   one ninety-nine

When the price is less than one dollar or euro, it is normal to say the currency.

80¢   eighty cents

Unit Vocabulary

Places

movie theater	bookstore	bus stop
supermarket	restaurant	bank
train station	parking lot	ATM
coffee shop	newsstand	
outdoor market	drugstore	

Coffee and other drinks

| orange juice | iced tea | coffee |
| bottled water | a cup of tea | |

Food

a chicken salad sandwich   a roast beef sandwich
a piece of chocolate cake   a house salad
a ham and cheese sandwich

Colors

| yellow | black | white | blue | red |
| orange | brown | green | pink | |

Clothes

| pair of shoes | coat | dress | T-shirt | shirt |
| pair of pants | skirt | sweater | blouse | hat |

UNIT 5
Things to see and do

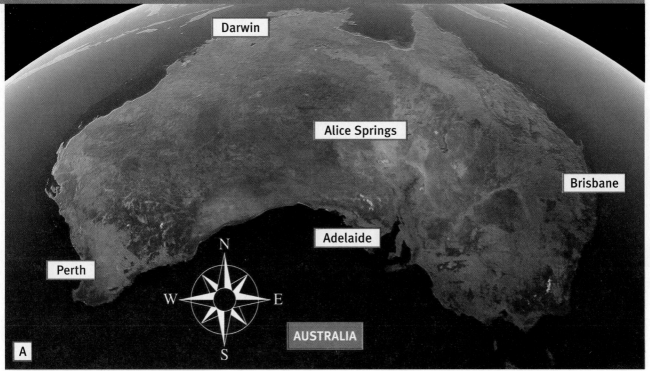

Darwin

Alice Springs

Brisbane

Adelaide

Perth

N
W E
S

AUSTRALIA

A

B

C

D

Warm Up

1a Match the places in picture A with the words in the box.

> south   north   west   east   center

1. Darwin = _____
2. Perth = _____
3. Brisbane = _____
4. Adelaide = _____
5. Alice Springs = _____

b ▶1.46 Listen and check your answers. Repeat the sentences.

2 **Pair Work** Talk about your country. What cities are in the north, south, east, west, and center of the country?

> *Seoul is in the north.*

3 Match photos B–D with a location.
_____ the city   _____ the country   _____ the coast

the White House

Pennsylvania Ave.

Constitution Ave.

5

4

Reading

1a **Pair Work** What is your favorite place to visit? Tell your partner.

> *My favorite place to visit is San Francisco.*

b Read the paragraph. Label the map with the <u>underlined</u> places in the paragraph.

2 **Pair Work** Take turns asking and answering the questions.

   1. Where is the White House?

   2. Where is the Washington Monument?

   3. Where is there a beautiful view?

   4. What is inside the Lincoln Memorial?

   5. What is on the Mall?

My favorite place to visit is Washington, D.C. The <u>White House</u> is near the center of the city. This beautiful old building is the home of the president. South of the White House there are a lot of monuments. The <u>Washington Monument</u> is tall and made of white marble. There is a beautiful view from the top. West of the Washington Monument is the <u>Lincoln Memorial</u>. There's a large statue of Lincoln inside. East of the Washington Monument is <u>the Mall</u>. There are a lot of museums there, and they are all free. There's also a beautiful red brick building, the <u>Smithsonian Castle</u>, on the south side of the Mall.

Speaking

3 **Pair Work** Read the How To box. What is important for a good vacation? Choose three things from the box below. Discuss.

> **How To:**
>
> **Give an opinion**
>
> I think . . .
>
> *I think beautiful beaches are important.*

great beaches	beautiful countryside	great outdoor activities	great tourist attractions
good shopping	beautiful buildings	good theaters and museums	good food

50

Vocabulary | *some, a lot of*

4a Match the pictures to the sentences.

_____ 1. There are *some* people in the theater.

_____ 2. There are *a lot of* people in the theater.

_____ 3. There's one person in the theater.

b ▶1.47 Listen. Check your answers. Then repeat.

A   B   C

Grammar | *there is/there are*: affirmative statements

5 Complete the Active Grammar box with *is* or *are*.

6 Complete the sentences with *There's* or *There are*.

1. _There's_____ a famous castle in Edinburgh.

2. _____ a great museum in Taipei.

3. _____ good restaurants in São Paolo.

4. _____ some beautiful beaches in Cancún.

5. _____ a lot of nice hotels in New York.

6. _____ a famous mountain near Tokyo.

Active Grammar

There	's	a large statue.
There	_____	a beautiful view.
There	_____	a lot of monuments.
		a lot of museums.

See Reference page 58

7 **Pair Work** Look at the map of greater Los Angeles. Talk about the tourist attractions.

> *There are some good museums.*

> *There is an outdoor market north of Venice City Beach.*

Writing

8a **Pair Work** Make notes about your favorite place to visit. Tell your partner.

> *There are a lot of good restaurants in the center of town.*

b Look at the Writing Bank on page 117.

c Read the paragraph in Exercise 1b again. Write a description of your favorite place to visit.

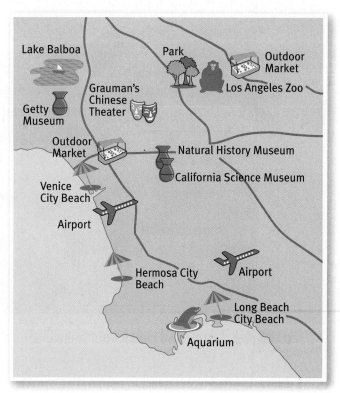

Lake Balboa
Getty Museum
Grauman's Chinese Theater
Outdoor Market
Venice City Beach
Airport
Park
Outdoor Market
Los Angeles Zoo
Natural History Museum
California Science Museum
Hermosa City Beach
Airport
Long Beach City Beach
Aquarium

Ask for and understand basic information about a new town

GRAMMAR *there is/there are*: negative statements and questions

Vocabulary | prepositions of location

1a Match the prepositions in the box to the pictures.

across from ~~in~~ on in front of near next to behind

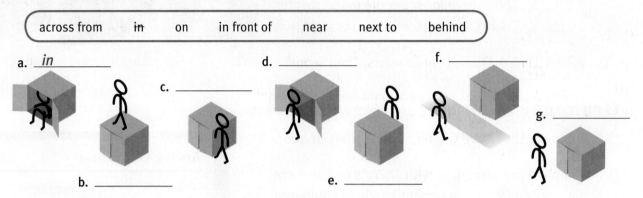

a. *in*_____

c. _____

d. _____

f. _____

g. _____

b. _____

e. _____

b Look at the map. Complete the sentences.

1. The bookstore is _____ the Italian restaurant.
2. The coffee shop is _____ the train station.
3. The drugstore is _____ the shoe store.
4. The theater is _____ the hotel.
5. The parking lot is _____ the department store.

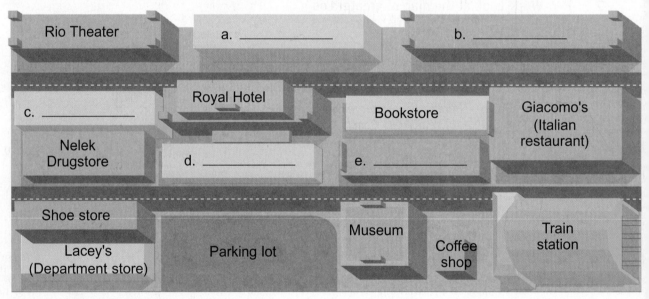

Rio Theater

a. _____

b. _____

c. _____

Royal Hotel

Bookstore

Giacomo's (Italian restaurant)

Nelek Drugstore

d. _____

e. _____

Shoe store

Museum

Train station

Lacey's (Department store)

Parking lot

Coffee shop

c ▶1.48 Listen and check your answers.

Listening

2a ▶1.49 Listen to people in the Royal Hotel ask for directions. Fill in the blanks in the map above.

b Listen again and look at the map. Mark these sentences true (*T*) or false (*F*). Correct the false sentences.

_____ 1. There are two coffee shops near the hotel.

_____ 2. There are four restaurants.

_____ 3. The bank is open today.

_____ 4. The ATM is near the hotel.

Grammar | *there is*/*there are*: negative statements and questions

3 Complete the Active Grammar box with *is*, *isn't*, *are*, or *aren't*.

4 Look at the map on page 52 again. Complete the sentences with *There isn't/aren't*.

1. <u>There aren't</u> any bus stops.
2. _____ a supermarket.
3. _____ any newsstands.
4. _____ a market.

Active Grammar

⊖	There	isn't (is not)	a bus stop near here.
⊖	There	_____ (are not)	any bookstores near here.
?	_____	there	a bank near here?
	Yes there is.		No, there _____.
?	Are	there	any hotels near here?
	Yes there _____.		No, there _____.

Use *any* for plurals in negatives and questions with *there is/are*.

See Reference page 58

Speaking

5 **SPEAKING EXCHANGE** Talk about places near a hotel.

Student A: You are a hotel receptionist. Look at page 111.

Student B: You are a hotel guest. Look at page 114.

Vocabulary | nationalities

6a Match the types of restaurants to the restaurant names below.

1. a French restaurant
2. an Italian restaurant
3. a Mexican restaurant
4. an Indian restaurant
5. a Chinese restaurant
6. a Japanese restaurant

___ LA SPIGA   ___ Azteca   ___ SUSHI TARO

_1_ Chez Pierre   ___ WONG LI   ___ The Taj Mahal

b ▶1.50 Listen and check your answers.

c **Group Work** What is your favorite kind of food? Use nationalities in your answers.

> My favorite is Italian food. It's great!

7 **Pair Work** Take turns asking and answering about places near your class.

> restaurants   drugstores   banks   department stores
> coffee shops   bookstores   theaters

> Are there any good Italian restaurants near here?

> Yes, there are. There's a great Italian restaurant across from the train station. Its called Roma. And . . .

Summer *English Plus!* Classes

Welcome to Hartford's Summer Program. Our *English Plus!* classes teach a skill in English. They are very popular with students from all over the world.

Class 171:	English + 	9:00 A.M.—11:00 A.M.
Class 172:	English +	4:00 P.M.—7:00 P.M.
Class 173:	English +	2:00 P.M.—4:00 P.M.
Class 174:	English +	9:00 A.M.—1:00 P.M.
Class 175:	English +	6:00 P.M.—8:00 P.M.
Class 176:	English +	10:00 A.M.—1:00 P.M.
Class 177:	English +	7:00 P.M.—10:00 P.M.
Class 178:	English +	1:00 P.M.—3:00 P.M.

Vocabulary | skills

1   **Pair Work** Look at the brochure above. Point to a symbol. Your partner says the word or phrase from the box.

> cook   play golf   drive   play the piano   swim   use a computer   sing   dance

Listening

2a   ▶1.51 Listen to Peter and Carla talk about summer classes at Hartford. Which class can Carla take?

b   Listen again. Write *Yes* or *No* next to each activity for Carla.

   Yes 1. drive   _____ 5. use a computer
   _____ 2. swim   _____ 6. dance
   _____ 3. play golf   _____ 7. sing
   _____ 4. cook   _____ 8. play the piano

3   **Pair Work** Read the How To box. Stand and greet your classmates.

> **How To:**
>
> **Greet a friend**
>
> **A:** *How are you?*
> **B:** *Fine/OK/Not bad, thanks. And you?*
> **A:** *Fine/OK/Not bad, thanks.*

Pronunciation | vowel clarity in *can* and *can't*

4a ▶1·52 Listen. Check (✓) the word you hear.

	can can't		can can't		can can't		can can't		can can't
1.	☐ ☐	2.	☐ ☐	3.	☐ ☐	4.	☐ ☐	5.	☐ ☐

b Listen again. Then repeat.

Grammar | *can/can't*: ability

5 Complete the Active Grammar box with *can* or *can't*.

6a Write sentences or questions using the cues.

1. (They/✗/dance) _They can't dance_ .
2. (you/swim?) _____ ?
3. (He/✓/speak Italian) _____ .
4. (she/drive?) _____ ?
5. (you/play golf?) _____ ?
6. (I/✗/play the piano) _____ .

Active Grammar

➕	I	can	swim, but
➖	I	_____	play golf.
❓	_____	you	cook? dance?
	Yes, I can. No, I can't.		

See Reference page 58

b **Pair Work** Ask your partner questions with the words from Exercise 1.

> Can you drive?

> Yes, I can. Can you drive?

Vocabulary | telling time

7 ▶1·53 Listen and repeat the times.

a. `10:00 A.M.`   b. `3:00 P.M.`   c. `7:00 P.M.`   d. `8:00 A.M.`   e. `1:00 P.M.`

8 **Pair Work** Say a time from the brochure in Exercise 1. Your partner tells you the class.

> Two o'clock to four o'clock in the afternoon.

> Class 173.

Speaking

9 **Group Work** Look at the job ads. Talk to your classmates. Find one person for each job.

NAME: _____

NAME: _____

NAME: _____

Review

1   Circle the correct word or words.

> The palace is in the center of town. There *is/are* (1.) a nice café near the palace, and there *is/are* (2.) two good restaurants, too. There are *a/some* (3.) beautiful buildings to the north of the palace, and there are *a/a lot* (4.) of tourist attractions to the south. There *is/are* (5.) a great museum to the west of the palace, and there are *one/some* (6.) nice hotels to the east.

2   Use the words to write sentences or questions.

1. any/your/Are/theaters/town/in/there
   Are there any theaters in your town ?

2. hotel/There/is/house/near/my/a/nice
   _____ .

3. a/of/the/in/lot/theater/are/There/people
   _____ .

4. aren't/here/any/restaurants/There/near
   _____ .

5. museums/Are/this/near/hotel/there/any
   _____ ?

6. next/There/bank/is/to/a/drugstore/this
   _____ .

3   Write questions and answers with *there*. Then take turns asking and answering the questions with a partner.

1. A: _Is there an Italian restaurant near here_ ? (Italian restaurant/near here)
   B: _Yes, there is_ . (Yes)

2. A: _Are there a lot of people in your hotel_ ? (a lot of people/in your hotel)
   B: _No, there aren' t_ . (No)

3. A: _____ ? (parking lot/in front of the hotel)
   B: _____ . (No)

4. A: _____ ? (any good beaches/near your hotel)
   B: _____ . (Yes)

5. A: _____ ? (Indian restaurant/on this street)
   B: _____ . (No)

6. A: _____ ? (any good department stores/near here)
   B: _____ . (Yes)

4   Complete the sentences with the words in the box.

> any   some   French   near   o'clock   use   play   ~~after~~

1. It's ten _after_ nine.
2. There's a really good _____ restaurant on East Street.
3. The pen is on the table _____ that book.
4. Are there _____ people in the theater?
5. Can you _____ a computer?
6. Breakfast is from eight _____ to ten thirty.
7. There are _____ people outside. Who are they?
8. He can't _____ golf, but she can.

Communication | check in to a bed and breakfast

5a What is a Bed and Breakfast (B&B)?

b **Pair Work** Which of the words in the box do you see in the pictures? Discuss.

> continental breakfast   croissants   hot tub   king-sized bed   mountain view

c ▶1·54 Listen to the conversation. Fill in the times below.

Hot Tub: open from _____ to _____
Breakfast: from _____ to _____
Checkout: _____

6a ▶1·55 Look at the clock. Listen and repeat.

b **Pair Work** Take turns saying the times.

1. 3:30	7. 6:20	13. 10:10
2. 5:15	8. 1:05	14. 9:40
3. 8:45	9. 9:35	15. 12:15
4. 11:30	10. 8:15	
5. 7:10	11. 2:25	
6. 7:45	12. 2:55	

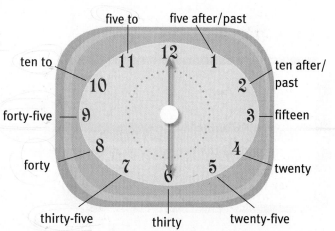

7 **Pair Work** Student A is the owner of a B&B.
Student B is a guest. Student A welcomes B. Show the guest the bedroom and hot tub. Talk about hot tub hours, breakfast times, and checkout. Then change roles.

> *Welcome to our B&B. This is your bedroom. There's a king-sized bed, and the bathroom is here.*

> *What time is checkout?*

Unit 5 Reference

there is/are

⊕	There's / There is	a bank near here.
⊖	There isn't	an aquarium near here.
⊕	There are	two outdoor markets. / some banks near here.
⊖	There aren't	any museums in town.
❓	Is there	a supermarket near here?
	Yes there is. No, there isn't.	
❓	Are there	any	tourist attractions near here?
	Yes there are. No, there aren't.	

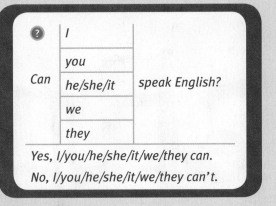

❓	Can	I / you / he/she/it / we / they	speak English?

Yes, I/you/he/she/it/we/they can.
No, I/you/he/she/it/we/they can't.

some/a lot of/any

Use *some* and *a lot of* in affirmative sentences with *There are* + plural nouns.

> There are **some** restaurants near the bank.

A lot of = a large number

> There are **a lot of** people in the bank.

Use *any* in negative sentences and questions with plurals.

> There aren't **any** hotels in this town.
> Are there **any** markets in this town?

Prepositions of place

in   behind   across from

on   in front of   next to   near

can/can't: ability

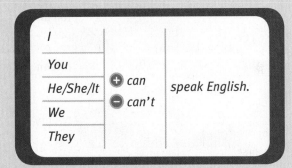

I / You / He/She/It / We / They	⊕ can / ⊖ can't	speak English.

Use *can* and *can't* before the verb to show ability.

Telling the time

06:00 six o' clock

06:15 six fifteen

06:40 six forty

06:10 ten after six

06:30 six thirty

06:45 six forty-five

Unit Vocabulary

Nationalities

Chinese	French	Indian	Italian
Japanese	Mexican	Korean	

Abilities

play the piano	dance	drive
play golf	swim	sing
use a computer	cook	

UNIT 6
All about you

A
B

C
D

Warm Up

1a ▶2.02 Listen to the adjectives in the box and repeat. Then check the meanings in a dictionary.

> sad   thin   tall   short   heavy   good-looking   young
> old   rich   ugly   poor   happy   intelligent

b **Pair Work** Say a word. Your partner says the opposite.   (Short.)   (Tall.)

2a Write the sentences in the box on the correct line.

> He's not very rich.   He's rich.   He's very rich.   ~~He's pretty rich.~~

➕➕➕ _____   ➕➕ _____   ➕ _He's pretty rich._ ➖ _____

b **Pair Work** Talk about the photos. Use the adjectives with *very, pretty,* or *not very.*

Say what you like/don't like

CAN DO ✓

GRAMMAR simple present: *I/you*; object pronouns

Listening

1a ▶2.03 Listen. What's João's favorite kind of music?

American English	British English
soccer	football

b Listen again. What does João like? Write ✓ or ✗ next to each word or phrase.

_____ 1. Chicago   _____ 3. Brazilian music   _____ 5. Indian food   _____ 7. German cars

_____ 2. soccer   _____ 4. hip hop music   _____ 6. French food   _____ 8. Italian fashion

Grammar | simple present: *I like*

2a Complete the Active Grammar box with *do* or *don't*.

b Complete the sentences with *like* or *don't like*.

1. ☹ I _*don't like*_ chicken.
2. ☺ I _____ Los Angeles.
3. ☹ I _____ Mondays.
4. ☺ I _____ vacations.

> ### Active Grammar
>
> | ⊕ | I | like | German cars. |
> |---|---|---|---|
> | ⊖ | I | don't like | hip hop music. |
> | ? | _____ you | like | soccer? |
> | | Yes, I _____. | | No, I _____. |

See Reference page 68

c Write questions for each of the sentences above.

1. _Do you like chicken?_   3. _____

2. _____   4. _____

Pronunciation | *yes/no* questions: intonation

3a ▶2.04 Listen. Does the intonation go up (↗) or down (↘) at the end?

b Listen again. Repeat.

Speaking

4 **Pair Work** Think of one thing or person you like and one thing or person you don't like for each category. Tell your partner and ask if he or she likes it.

- food
- famous people
- sports teams
- cars
- music
- time of day
- colors
- places

> I like Italian food. Do you like Italian food?

> Yes, I do. I don't like salad. Do you like salad?

Grammar | object pronouns: *me/you/him/her/it/us/them*

5a ▶2.05 Match a sentence to a picture. Then listen and check your answers.

  a. I don't like <u>her</u>.   c. I like <u>them</u>.   e. I like <u>you</u>.

  b. ~~Do you like <u>me</u>?~~   d. I don't like <u>him</u>.   f. I like <u>it</u>.

1. _b_   2. ____   3. ____   4. ____   5. ____   6. ____

b Complete the chart with the underlined words in Exercise 5a.

Subject pronoun	Object pronoun	Subject pronoun	Object pronoun
I		we	us
you			
he/she/it		they	

Speaking

6a Read the How To box.

b Work in pairs.

    Student A: Look at the list below.

    Student B: Look at the list on page 112 in the Speaking Exchange.

How To:
Say when you don't understand
A: *Do you like Salma Hayek?*
B: *Sorry?/Pardon?/Who's Salma Hayek?*
A: *She's an actress.*
B: *Oh, yes. I like her.*

1. Tom Cruise   3. beautiful beaches   5. instant coffee   7. golf

2. Salma Hayek   4. department stores   6. Brad Pitt and Angelina Jolie   8. baseball

c Read your list to your partner. Your partner says *I like/don't like* + object pronoun.

> Tom Cruise.

> I don't like him.

7 **Pair Work** Do a 60-second interview with your partner. Use your questions from Exercise 4. Think of eight new questions. Use:

> Do you like . . . ?

> Who's/What's your favorite . . . ?

Have a conversation with someone you don't know

GRAMMAR simple present: *we/they*; *wh-* questions: *who/what/where*

Vocabulary | jobs and activities

1a Match the jobs in the box to the pictures.

> ____ architect   ____ fashion designer   ____ reporter
>
> ____ sales rep   ____ construction worker   ____ chef

a.   b.   c.   d.   e.   f.

b ▶2.06 Write a verb from the box below in each blank. Then listen and check your answers.

> sell   write   build   cook   design (x2)

1. Architects _design_ buildings.
2. Sales reps _____ things.
3. Fashion designers _____ clothes.
4. Reporters _____ articles.
5. Chefs _____ food.
6. Construction workers _____ buildings.

Listening

2a ▶2.07 Listen to four people at a hotel in China. Match the jobs from Exercise 1a to the people in the photo.

Anthony _____
Catherine _____
Sharon _____
Pat _____

b Listen again. Mark the sentences true (*T*) or false (*F*).

Sharon and Pat

____ 1. They live in the US.

____ 2. They are there on business.

____ 3. They design houses and office buildings.

Catherine and Anthony

____ 4. They are there on vacation.

____ 5. They live in Canada.

____ 6. PDS Fashions is a small company.

Grammar 1 | simple present: *we/they*

3a Complete the Active Grammar box with *do* or *don't*.

b Are the sentences below true for you?
Write *Yes* or *No* next to them.

_____ 1. I like American movies.

_____ 2. I like Italian food.

_____ 3. I like British music.

_____ 4. I live near this school.

_____ 5. I like soccer.

_____ 6. I like sushi.

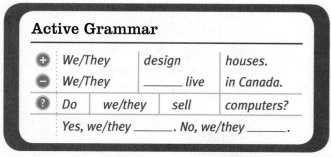

Active Grammar			
⊕ We/They	design		houses.
⊖ We/They	_____	live	in Canada.
? Do	we/they	sell	computers?
Yes, we/they _____. No, we/they _____.			

See Reference page 68

c **Pair Work** Make sentences about things that are true for both you and your partner.

> *We both don't like American movies.*

Grammar 2 | *wh-* questions: *who/what/where*

4 Complete the Active Grammar box with *Who, What,* or *Where*.

5 Write questions from the Active Grammar box for each answer below.

1. A: *What do you do* _____ ?
   B: I'm a designer.

2. A: _____ ?
   B: I work in Paris.

3. A: _____ ?
   B: I work for GT Designs.

4. A: _____ ?
   B: I design cars.

Active Grammar			
What	do	you	do?
_____	do	you	work/live?
_____	do	you	sell/design/write?
_____	do	you	work for?

See Reference page 68

6 **Pair Work** Read the How To box. Stand and ask other students questions from the Active Grammar box.

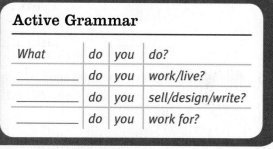

How To:
Show interest
A: *I'm a fashion designer/sales rep, etc.*
B: *Oh really?/Great!/Interesting. What do you build/design/sell, etc.?*

Speaking

7 **SPEAKING EXCHANGE** Work in groups of four as two pairs.

Students A and B: Read your details on page 110.

Students C and D: Read your details on page 112.

You are at a club in San Francisco. Have a conversation with the other pair. Use the questions from the Active Grammar box.

Talk about the routines of people you know

GRAMMAR simple present: *he/she/it*; short answers

Vocabulary | daily activities

1a Read the sentences. Write the correct <u>underlined</u> verb phrase under each picture.

1. I <u>get up</u> at 11 o'clock.
2. I <u>take a shower</u> every day.
3. I <u>eat hamburgers</u> for dinner.
4. I <u>start work</u> at nine.
5. I <u>finish work</u> at nine o'clock.
6. I <u>eat a salad</u> for breakfast.
7. I <u>watch TV</u> at night.
8. I don't <u>go to bed</u> early.

a.

1. get up

b.

_____

c.

_____

d.

_____

e.

_____

f.

_____

g.

_____

h.

_____

b **Pair Work** Change the sentences in Exercise 1a to make them true for you. Tell your partner.

> *I get up at seven.*

Reading

2a Read Emma's essay. Complete the sentences.

1. Mei is Emma's _____ .
2. Frank is Emma's _____ .
3. Roberta is Emma's _____ .
4. Adam is Emma's _____ .

b **Pair Work** Ask and answer questions with *Yes, he/she does*, or *No, he/she doesn't*.

1. Does Frank take a shower every day?
2. Does Adam get up at eight o'clock?
3. Does Mei eat fast food?
4. Does Roberta start work at eight thirty?
5. Does Frank eat fast food for breakfast?
6. Does Mei watch TV?

Emma

Mei is my best friend. She's a yoga teacher. She's not rich, but she's happy. She eats salad every day. She doesn't eat fast food, and she doesn't watch TV.

Frank is my brother and he's a biker. He's pretty tall and very intelligent. He eats fast food for breakfast every day. He doesn't take a shower every day.

Roberta is my aunt. She's a sales rep. She starts work at eight thirty in the morning, and she finishes work at nine o'clock at night. She's not a happy person.

Adam is a musician. He gets up at 11 o'clock in the morning, and he goes to bed at 2 o'clock in the morning. He's not very intelligent — but it's OK — he's good-looking and he's my husband. I love him!

Grammar | simple present: *he/she/it*

3 Look at Emma's essay in Exercise 2a on page 64 again. Complete the Active Grammar box.

Active Grammar

⊕	He/She/It	start___	work at eight thirty.
		finish___	work at nine o'clock.
⊖	He/She/It	_____ eat	fast food.
		_____ like	salad.
?	Does	he	get up	at nine?
		she	eat	breakfast early?

Yes, he/she/it does. No, he/she/it doesn't.

See Reference page 68

4a Complete the paragraph with the correct form of the words in the box.

> start   get   like   ~~work~~   finish   watch   eat (x2)

My best friend is Koji. He's a chef in a French restaurant. He __works__ (1.) in the evening, so he _____ (2.) up around ten or eleven o'clock in the morning. He _____ (3.) breakfast and lunch together – it's called "brunch". He _____ (4.) TV in the afternoon, and he _____ (5.) work around four o'clock. He _____ (6.) dinner at work. He _____ (7.) work around midnight. He _____ (8.) his job.

Koji

b Fill in the blanks with the correct form of the words in parentheses.

1. He _doesn't___ _like_____ this music. (not like)
2. _____ they _____ here? (work)
3. What _____ he _____? (do)
4. Sarah _____ _____ a lot of emails. (not write)

Writing

5a Complete each sentence below with the name of a friend or family member.

1. _____ is my best friend.
2. _____ is my favorite family member.

b Make notes about each person.

- What does he or she do? (**Ex:** He's a teacher.)
- What adjectives describe him or her? (**Ex:** She's young, happy.)
- What are his or her routines? (**Ex:** He gets up at eight o'clock.)

c Look at the Writing Bank on page 118. Write a paragraph about each person above.

Review

1 Complete each sentence or question with *me, you, him, her, it, us,* or *them.*

1. She's really nice. Do you like ___*her*___?
2. I don't like this show. Do you like _____?
3. Bill and Jenny aren't my friends. I don't like _____.
4. I really like him, but I don't think he likes _____.
5. You are great! I think he likes _____.
6. He's my friend. I like _____.
7. We like them, but do they like _____?

2 Complete the questions with *What, Where,* or *Who.* Then work with a partner and ask and answer the questions with true information.

1. A: ___*Where*___ do you live?
   B: In San Francisco.
2. A: _____ do you work for?
   B: A small software company.
3. A: _____ do you do?
   B: I'm a sales rep.
4. A: _____ do you sell?
   B: I sell computer software.
5. A: _____ do you work?
   B: In Silicon Valley.

3 Fill in the blanks with the correct form of the verb in parentheses.

Hi Victor,

How are you? I'm fine, but my new roommate is a problem. His name is Oscar. He's a designer. He ___*designs*___ (1. design/✓) shoes. He ___*doesn't get up*___ (2. get up/✗) until 11 o'clock every day. He _____ (3. take a shower/✗). He _____ (4. eat/✗) breakfast, but he _____ (5. watch/✓) TV for two or three hours. Then he _____ (6. start/✓) work at about two o'clock in the afternoon. He _____ (7. work/✗) in an office— he _____ (8. work/✓) at home. He _____ (9. finish/✓) work at about six o'clock. That's just four hours! He _____ (10. go/✓) to bed at three o'clock in the morning.

What can I do?

Love, Julia

4 Use the words to write complete sentences.

1. I/not like/French food
   I don't like French food .

2. She/get up/at 8 o'clock
   _____ .

3. they/start work/early
   _____ ?

4. Thomas/not eat/salad
   _____ .

5. Kim/watch TV/every day
   _____ ?

6. Paul and I/write/articles for *Newsmag*
   _____ .

7. Where/Carlos/live
   _____ ?

8. Jo and Alex/not go to bed/late
   _____ .

Communication | ask and answer questions about a friend

Find a nice present

my account | track order | quick order | help

Search ☐ GO

Information

Name?	Luz
Age?	29
Occupation?	Reporter
Company?	Newstime Magazine
Work long hours?	
Married?	
Have children?	
Travel a lot?	
Can cook?	
Watch a lot of movies?	
Listen to a lot of music?	

Present Ideas

1
2
3
4
5
6
7
8
9

---

5 Match nine words in the box to the pictures on the website above.

> ___ tie   ___ DVD   ___ book   ___ flowers   ___ suitcase   ___ MP3 player   ___ cookbook
> ___ CD   ___ bag   ___ pens   ___ wallet   ___ candles   ___ travel iron   ___ saucepans

6 ▶2.08 Listen to Part 1 of the conversation. What is the problem?

7a ▶2.09 Listen to Part 2 of the conversation. Answer the questions on the website for Jim's friend, Luz. Write *Yes* or *No* in the boxes.

b What are three good presents for Luz?

8 **SPEAKING EXCHANGE** Find a present for a friend.

    Student A: Close your book. Think of a friend.

    Student B: Look at the chart on page 113. Ask questions to find a good present for Student A's friend. Then change roles.

Unit 6 Reference

Simple present

+			
I	live		
You	work		
He			in Chicago.
She	lives		near my brother.
It	works		next to a bank.
We	live		
They	work		

With *he*, *she*, and *it*, add *-s* to the verb.

−			
I	don't	like	
You		eat	
He		like	chicken.
She	doesn't		coffee.
It		eat	salad.
We	don't	like	
They		eat	

?			
Do	I	design	
	you	write	
Does	he	design	books?
	she	write	
	it		
Do	we	design	
	they	write	

Yes, I/you/we/they do.
Yes, he/she/it does.

No, I/you/we/they don't.
No, he/she/it doesn't.

What do you design?

Where do you live?

Who do you like?

For verbs ending in *-ch*, *-sh*, *-ss*, and *-o*, add *-es* to the verb with *he*, *she*, and *it*: *He/She/It watches*

I	eat breakfast.
You	go to work.
We	finish work early.
They	watch TV.
He	eats breakfast.
She	goes to work.
	finishes work early.
It	watches TV.

Object pronouns

Object pronouns are the object of a verb. They come after the verb.

Subject pronouns	Object pronouns
I/you/he/she/it/we/they	me/you/him/her/it/us/them

*Do you like **me**?*   *I like **you**.*   *We like **him**.*

*He likes **her**.*   *She likes **it**.*   *They like **us**.*

*I like **them**.*

Unit Vocabulary

Adjectives

tall	ugly	poor	happy	young
sad	rich	heavy	intelligent	
old	thin	short	good-looking	

Jobs and activities

architects design buildings
construction workers build buildings
fashion designers design clothes
reporters write articles   chefs cook food
sales reps sell things

Daily activities

get up	eat breakfast	start work
go to bed	take a shower	finish work
watch TV	eat a salad	

Use *not very* to make negative descriptions more polite:

*She's **not very** intelligent.*

*They're **not very** rich.*

UNIT 7
A day at work

A

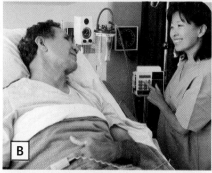
B

C

D

Warm Up

1 Match each photo or picture to a word in the box.

> ____ office ____ store ____ factory ____ restaurant
> ____ lab ____ school ____ hospital ____ university

E

F

G

H

2a Match an occupation to a photo or picture.

____ 1. a waiter

____ 2. an office worker

____ 3. a factory worker

____ 4. a nurse

____ 5. a sales clerk

____ 6. a professor

____ 7. a researcher

____ 8. a teacher

b ▶ 2.10 Listen and check your answers.

Understand simple instructions

GRAMMAR imperatives

CAN DO ✓

Listening and Vocabulary

1a ▶ **2.11** Listen. Who are the people in the pictures? Where are they?

b Listen again. Write a conversation number next to each phrase below.

  _2_ a. Please <u>sit down</u>.   ____ d. <u>Turn off</u> your cell phone.   ____ f. <u>Look at</u> page 32.

  ____ b. <u>Hold on</u>, please.   ____ e. <u>Listen to</u> the conversation.   ____ g. <u>Come in</u>.

  ____ c. <u>Be</u> quiet.

c Write an underlined phrase from Exercise 1b under its picture below.

1. _listen to_   2. _____   3. _____   4. _____

5. _____   6. _____   7. _____

Grammar | imperatives

2 Write a phrase from Exercise 1b in the Active Grammar box.

3 Fill in the blanks with a word or phrase from the box.

> Turn off   ~~Don't be~~   Speak   Use   Don't text

1. _Don't be_ late.
2. _____ English in class.
3. _____ your friends.
4. _____ your cell phone.
5. _____ a good dictionary.

Active Grammar

➕ Be quiet.

  _____ at page 45.

➖ Don't _____ in.

  Don't _____ down.

Use *please* to make an imperative polite.

Please *be quiet./Be quiet,* ***please.***
Please *don't look at my email./*
Don't look at my email, ***please.***

See Reference page 78

4 ▶2.12 Listen. Match each imperative to a place below.

_____ a. hospital _____ b. store _____ c. airport _1_ d. restaurant _____ e. school

5 **Pair Work** What are ways to improve your English? Write imperatives.

> Speak English every day.

Speaking

6a Read the How To box.

b **Group Work** Work in groups of three. Use the How To box to practice phone calls. Use the names below. Change roles each time.

> 1. Company = JK Designs
>   A = Paul Walker   B = Receptionist
>   C = Ken Noda
> 2. Company = Budget Construction
>   A = Angelo Romano   B = Receptionist
>   C = Sally Wood
> 3. Company = Renzo Rogers Architects
>   A = Helen Davis   B = Receptionist
>   C = Eduardo Medina

How To:

Make a business phone call

Use *My name's* with people you don't know.
Use *It's* with people you know.
B: *Hello. Parkside School.*
A: *Can I speak to Mrs. Fisher, please?*
B: *Hold on, please.*
C: *Hello. Alice Fisher.*
A: *Hello, Mrs. Fisher. My name's Jake Parker./It's Jake.*

Reading

7 Read the article. Answer the questions.

1. What time does Tim start work?
2. What does Tim do between 8 A.M. and 9 A.M.?
3. Where does Tim have lunch?
4. What does Tim do between 3:30 P.M. and 6 P.M.?
5. What time does Tim finish work?
6. When does Tim have a long vacation?

Tim Clark —a teacher in the US

I start work at 8:00. I check homework and prepare lessons. I teach from 9:00 to 12:30. I eat lunch in my classroom—a sandwich or a salad.

In the afternoon, I teach from 1:30 to 3:30. After school, I teach football or I work in my classroom. I go home at 6:00 and I eat dinner. After dinner, I check homework and prepare lessons. I finish work at 9:30. Teachers work a lot, but we have a long vacation in July* and August.

* for help with months, look at Exercise 8a

Vocabulary | months

8a ▶2.13 Listen and read the months. Then listen and repeat.

January	February	March	April	May	June
July	August	September	October	November	December

b Look at the pictures of New York City on page 111 in the Speaking Exchange. Guess the month.

c **Pair Work** Complete the sentences with months. Explain.

1. My favorite month is . . .   2. I don't like . . .

> *My favorite month is June. It's warm, but it's not very hot.*

Say how often you do something

GRAMMAR adverbs of frequency

Vocabulary | work phrases

1a **Group Work** What jobs (occupations) can you remember? Write a list.

b Look at the work phrases in the box. Match each picture to a phrase in the box.

> ____ attend meetings ____ write reports ____ give presentations ____ call customers
>
> _1_ travel for work ____ help people ____ answer the phone ____ work outdoors

| 1 | 2 | 3 | 4 |
| 5 | 6 | 7 | 8 |

Listening

2a ▶ 2.14 Listen to the *What's your job?* game. Check (✓) Yes or No in the chart below.

b Listen again. Complete the conversation with the words or phrases in the box.

> always (x2)   usually   not often
> often (x2)   never   sometimes (x2)

WHAT'S YOUR JOB?

	Yes	No
attend meetings	✓	___
give presentations	___	___
call customers	___	___
write reports	___	___
travel for work	___	___
answer the phone	___	___
work outdoors	___	___
help people	___	___

H: Hi, John. Are you ready?

J: Yes, I'm _always_ (1.) ready!

H: OK, let's start. Do you attend meetings?

J: Yes, I _____ (2.) attend meetings.

H: Do you give presentations?

J: Yes, I _____ (3.) give presentations.

H: Do you call customers?

J: Yes, I _____ (4.) call customers.

H: Do you write reports?

J: Yes, I do, but I _____ (5.) write reports.

H: Do you travel for work?

J: Yes, I _____ (6.) travel for work.

H: Do you answer the phone?

J: Yes, I _____ (7.) answer the phone.

H: Do you work outside?

J: No, I _____ (8.) work outside.

H: Do you help people?

J: Yes, I _____ (9.) help people.

H: Are you a . . . sales rep?

J: Yes, I am!

Grammar | adverbs of frequency

3 Look at the conversation in Exercise 2b again. Complete the Active Grammar box.

4 **Pair Work** Take turns making sentences about your daily routines. Use a phrase from the box and an adverb of frequency.

> get up   go to bed   start work
> watch TV   finish work   take a shower
> eat (something for) breakfast/lunch/dinner

> *I usually get up at seven o'clock.*

Active Grammar

```
100%    always
           usually
              often
                 sometimes
                    not often/not usually
   0%        never
```

1. verb *be* + adverb of frequency

   I'_____ _____ ready!

2. adverb of frequency + verb

   I _____ attend meetings.

   I don't often write reports.

See Reference page 78

Pronunciation | word stress

5a ▶ **2.15** Listen. Mark the stress.

1. <u>al</u>ways   2. usually   3. often   4. sometimes   5. never

b Listen again. Then repeat.

Speaking

6 **Pair Work** Take turns asking and answering questions about jobs.

Student A: Choose a job (or use your own).

Student B: Ask questions. Guess Student A's job.

> *Do you write reports?*   *Yes, I sometimes write reports.*

Writing

7 Read the notes and the How To box. Then write a request to Benita.

1.
> Hi Uma,
> Can you answer my phone this afternoon?
> There is a meeting at two o'clock.
> Thanks,
> Guy

2.
> Anna,
> I'm at home today. Can you call me? I have some questions for you.
> Many thanks,
> Emi

> Hello Benita,

> **How To:**
>
> **Write a request note**
>
> Start: (Hello/Hi) Jay,
> Request: Can you (please) + [request]?
> Finish: Thanks,/Many thanks, + [your name].

Listening

1a **Pair Work** Take turns saying the months of the year.

(January) (February) (March)

b ▶2.16 Listen and write on the calendar:

1. today 2. Mr. Wu 3. Mrs. King 4. Ms. Brown 5. Mr. Rodriguez

June

mon	tues	wed	thur	fri	sat	sun
		1	2	3	4	5
6	7	8	9	10	11	12
13	14	15	16	17	18	19
20	21	22	23	24	25	26
27	28	29	30			

Vocabulary | ordinal numbers

2a ▶2.17 Look at the calendar again. Listen and repeat the ordinal numbers.

b **Pair Work** Look at the calendar above. Take turns saying the ordinal numbers.

3 Read the How To box.

4 **Pair Work** Stand and talk to your classmates. Ask and answer about birthdays.

(When is your birthday?) (It's on . . .)

How To:

Write and say dates

Say *-th* after the number (except for *first*, *second*, and *third*).

Write	Say
September 1 / 9.1	September first
July 2 / 7.2	July second
April 3 / 4.3	April third
January 15 / 1.15	January fifteenth

See Reference page 78

Grammar | *would like:* preferences and offers

5a ▶2.18 Read and listen to the conversation. Fill in the blanks.

Michelle:	Please come in. Have a seat. What would you like <u>to</u> (1.) drink? Tea? Coffee?
Mr. Rodriguez:	I'd like coffee.
Ms. Khan:	I'd _____ (2.) a cup of tea, please.
Michelle:	Would you like milk or sugar?
Mr. Rodriguez:	No, thank you.
Ms. Khan:	Milk, no sugar, please.

b **Group Work** Practice the conversation in groups of three. Change roles.

6 Complete the Active Grammar box with *would* or *'d.*

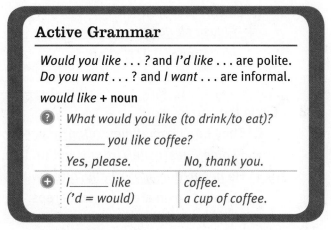

Active Grammar

Would you like . . . ? and *I'd like . . .* are polite.
Do you want . . . ? and *I want . . .* are informal.

would like + noun

? What would you like (to drink/to eat)?

_____ you like coffee?

Yes, please.	No, thank you.
+ I _____ like	coffee.
('d = would)	a cup of coffee.

See Reference page 78

Speaking

7 **Pair Work** Practice welcoming visitors.

Student A: You are a visitor. **Student B:** Welcome Student A. Offer drinks and snacks.

> *Hello, Mrs. Lee. My name is Pedro García.*   *Nice to meet you, Mr. García.*   *Please, come in.*

Vocabulary | food and drink

8 Match the words in the box to the pictures below.

___ soup	___ desserts
___ fruit	___ appetizers
___ salad	___ vegetables
___ drinks	___ main courses
___ snacks	

Listening

9 ▶2.19 Listen to Michelle, Mr. Rodriguez, and Ms. Khan. Fill in the blanks on the map of the company cafeteria.

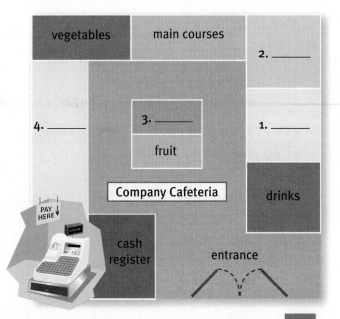

Review

1   Use the words to write imperatives.

1. down/Please/sit
   Please sit down.

2. your/phone/cell/Turn off

3. late/don't/Please/be

4. at/look/50/page/Please

2   Circle the correct word.

1. They don't *sometimes/often/never* give presentations.

2. I *sometimes/never/usually* get up late. I get up at 6 o'clock every day.

3. He *never/doesn' t usually/often* works late. He's a manager and he has a lot of work.

4. Tom and Kevin are good sales reps. They *always/never/sometimes* listen to their customers.

3   Use the word in parentheses to write a sentence.

1. Francis helps people. (always)
   Francis always helps people.

2. I attend meetings on Mondays. (sometimes)

3. She doesn't watch TV in the evening. (usually)

4. He is late for work. (never)

5. You aren't home in the evening. (usually)

6. We don't write reports. (often)

4   Match each question to a reply. Then practice asking and answering the questions with a partner.

1. What would you like to eat?
2. What would you like to drink?
3. Would you like coffee?
4. Would you like milk or sugar?

a. I'd like bottled water, please.
b. I'd like a salad, please.
c. Milk, no sugar, please.
d. Yes, please.

5   Complete each phrase or list with another word. Then share your answers with a partner.

1. March, April, _May_
2. appetizer, main course, _____
3. hold _____
4. a factory _____
5. June, July, _____
6. answer the _____
7. milk or _____
8. September, October, _____
9. a student, a teacher, _____
10. a fashion _____
11. fifth, sixth, _____
12. nineteenth, twentieth, _____

Communication | get and give directions in a building

6 **Pair Work** Talk about the different floors of the building.

> *What floor are the sales reps on?*

> *They're on the fourth floor.*

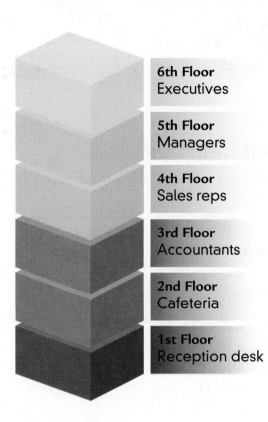

6th Floor
Executives

5th Floor
Managers

4th Floor
Sales reps

3rd Floor
Accountants

2nd Floor
Cafeteria

1st Floor
Reception desk

3rd Floor

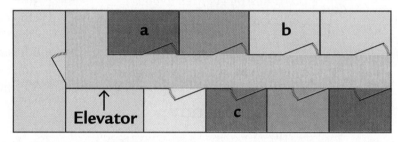

a   b

↑
Elevator   c

7a Who says the phrases below, the receptionist (*R*) or the visitor (*V*)?

_____ 1. I'm here to see . . .

_____ 2. Do you have an appointment?

_____ 3. What's your name, please?

_____ 4. How do you spell that?

_____ 5. Take the elevator to the third floor.

_____ 6. Thank you.

_____ 7. You're welcome.

b ▶2.20 Listen and check your answers.

8 Listen again. Match the places below to the letters on the floor plan.

_____ 1. Martina Hafner's office

_____ 2. Lorda Romero's office

_____ 3. Patrick Swinton's office

9 **Pair Work** Practice giving directions in a building. Change roles.

Student A: You are the receptionist. Think of the name of someone who works in the building. Write it on the floor plan. Tell your partner the name.

Student B: You are a visitor. Listen to the name Student A tells you. You have a meeting with this person. Act out the conversation.

> *Good morning.*

> *Good morning. I have a meeting with . . .*

Unit 7 Reference

Imperatives

➕	Be quiet. Sit down.
➖	Don't talk. Don't sit down.

Affirmative imperatives

(Please) | Sit down.
Turn off your cell phone.
Look at page 32.
Come in.

Negative imperatives

(Please) | Don't sit down.
Don't turn off your cell phone.
Don't look at page 32.
Don't come in.

Use *please* to make the imperative more polite.

Adverbs of frequency

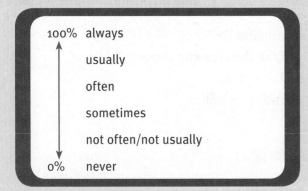

100%	always
	usually
	often
	sometimes
	not often/not usually
0%	never

Adverbs of frequency come **after** the verb *be*.
> She's **always** late.
> They're **never** happy.

Adverbs of frequency come **before** other verbs.
> He **doesn't often** give presentations.
> We **don't usually** eat desserts.

Would you like . . . ? I'd like . . .

Use *would like* to offer food or drink to guests.
> What **would** you **like**?
> What **would** you **like** to drink?
> **Would** you **like** coffee?
> Yes, please./No, thank you.

Use *I'd like* . . . to say what you prefer.
> **I'd like** a cup of tea, please.
> **I'd like** an appetizer, please.

Ordinal numbers

Add *-th* to make most ordinal numbers (except for first, second, and third).

1st	first	9th	ninth	17th	seventeenth
2nd	second	10th	tenth	18th	eighteenth
3rd	third	11th	eleventh	19th	nineteenth
4th	fourth	12th	twelfth	20th	twentieth
5th	fifth	13th	thirteenth	21st	twenty-first
6th	sixth	14th	fourteenth	22nd	twenty-second
7th	seventh	15th	fifteenth		
8th	eighth	16th	sixteenth		

Dates

Writing dates		Saying dates
August 21	*8.21*	*August twenty-first*

Unit Vocabulary

Work places

office	factory	hospital	university
store	school	cafeteria	lab

Months

January	April	July	October
February	May	August	November
March	June	September	December

Work phrases

attend meetings	give presentations
work outdoors	call customers
write reports	travel for work
answer the phone	

Food

fruit	soup	appetizers	desserts
drinks	salad	vegetables	snacks
main courses			

Your likes and dislikes

Warm Up

1a Match each leisure activity in the box to its picture below.

go biking	go out to eat	play chess	go hiking	play tennis	go sightseeing
work out	read a book	play soccer	watch TV	go swimming	~~go to the theater~~

1. _go to the theater_

4. _____

7. _____

10. _____

2. _____

5. _____

8. _____

11. _____

3. _____

6. _____

9. _____

12. _____

b ▶ 2.21 Listen and check. Then repeat.

2 **Pair Work** How often do you do these activities? Tell your partner.

Speaking

1a Look at the destinations.
What can you see in the photos?

b Read the How To box. What activities can you do at each destination?

2 **Group Work** What's a nice place you like to visit? What can you do there?

> **How To:**
>
> **Talk about things to do**
>
> Use *You can . . .* or *We can . . .* to talk about things to do in a place.
>
> *You can play golf in Palm Springs.*
>
> *We can go sightseeing in San Francisco.*

Listening

3a ▶2.22 Listen. What is Gary and Annie's problem?

b ▶2.23 Listen. Complete the sentences.
  1. Gary wants to go to _____.   3. They both want to go to _____.
  2. Annie wants to go to _____.

Pronunciation | reduction of sounds: *want to*

4a ▶2.24 Listen. How is *want to* pronounced in these sentences?

b Listen again. Then repeat.

Grammar | *like* + gerund/infinitive; *want* + infinitive

5 Complete the Active Grammar box with *want* or *like*. Check Audioscript 2.23 on page 127 for help.

Active Grammar

➕ I _____ playing (or to play) golf.	➕ I _____ to go sightseeing.
➖ I don't like going (or to go) sightseeing.	➖ I don't want to play golf.

See Reference page 88

6 Circle the correct forms of the verb to complete the sentences.

1. I like (*going out*) (*to go out*) with friends.
2. Gary doesn't want *watching* / (*to watch*) TV.
3. Do you want *playing* / *to play* tennis?
4. We like *going* / *to go* sightseeing.
5. She doesn't want *going out* / *to go out* to eat.
6. Do they like *playing* / *to play* chess?
7. I don't like *swimming* / *to go swimming*.
8. Martin wants *reading* / *to read* now.

Vocabulary | adjectives

7 Match each word in the box to its situation below.

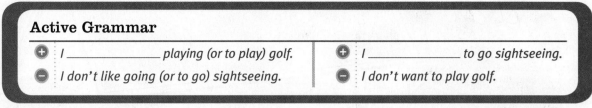

boring ~~exciting~~ fun
difficult interesting easy

1.

This is really _exciting_ .

3.

This is _____ .

5.

This is very _____ .

2.

This is very _____ .

4.

This is _____ .

6.

This is really _____ .

Speaking

8 **Group Work** Choose a destination from Exercise 1a for next weekend. Stand and find other students to go with you.

Writing

9 Look at the Writing Bank on page 119. Then write an email to a hotel in one of the destinations in Exercise 1a.

Say what things you possess CAN DO ✓

GRAMMAR *have/has*

Vocabulary | rooms and furniture

1a **Pair Work** Look at the house. Ask and answer questions. Where do you:

a. cook? b. watch TV? c. take a shower? d. go to bed? e. park your car? f. play soccer?

Where do you cook?   *I cook in the kitchen.*

b Match the words in the box to the items in the picture.

✓ dishwasher	___ sofa	___ bed	___ bicycle	___ bathtub	___ wardrobe
___ coffee table	___ lamp	___ car	___ cabinet	___ window	___ armchair
___ mirror	___ toilet	___ sink	___ fridge	___ stove	

American English	British English
stove	cooker

c ▶2.25 Listen and check your answers. Then listen and repeat.

Listening

2a ▶2.26 Listen. Which items from Exercise 1b do you hear? Circle them.

b Listen again. Put a check (✓) next to the things in Exercise 1b that Pablo's sister has.

c Look at Jo's suggestion for a wedding present on page 111 in the Speaking Exchange. Do you think it's a good idea? Why or why not?

Grammar | *have/has*

3a Look at Audioscript 2.26 on page 127. <u>Underline</u> examples of *have* and *has*.

b Complete the Active Grammar box with *have, has, do,* or *does*.

4 **Pair Work** Ask your partner questions with the words in Exercise 1b.

> Do you have any armchairs?

> Yes, I do. I have two armchairs in my living room, and I have one armchair in my bedroom.

Active Grammar

I You We They	⊕	_____	a bicycle.
	⊖	don't _____	a sofa.
			a yard.
He She It	⊕	_____	a garage.
	⊖	doesn't _____	
❓		_____	I/you/we/they have	a bicycle?
❓		_____	he/she/it have	an armchair?

Yes, I/you/we/they _____. Yes, he/she/it _____.
No, I/you/we/they _____. No, he/she/it _____.

See Reference page 88

Speaking

5 **Pair Work** Find a new partner. Talk about your house, apartment, or bedroom.

> My family has an apartment. It's pretty big. I have a small bedroom. I have a TV and a computer in my bedroom, but I don't have . . .

Reading

6 **SPEAKING EXCHANGE** Do the *Technology* quiz on page 113. Ask your partner the questions and write his or her answers.

> Do you have an e-book reader?

> No, I don't, but I want one.

7a Add your points and find your score.

b **Pair Work** Read your score results. Are the score results true? Discuss with your partner.

A = 2 points   B = 1 point   C = 0 points

0–6 points: You don't like new technology; you like old things. Your photographs are on paper, not on your computer. You use a map—you don't use a GPS device. Your television is quite old. You don't like to spend money on new technology.

7–12 points: You like new technology and you sometimes buy new things. You sometimes read about new technology in newspapers and magazines. You take a lot of digital photos.

13–18 points: You really like new technology. You have the newest cell phone. You often read about new technology in newspapers and magazines. You like to spend money on new technology.

Suggest a restaurant; make reservations; order food

CAN DO ✓

GRAMMAR *wh-* question words: *which/how*

Listening

1a ▶2.27 Listen to Mark and Anna. Which restaurant do they want to go to?

_____ a. Sinatra's _____ b. Wasabi _____ c. Carlito's

b Listen again. Number the questions in the order you hear them.

_____ Where's that?

_____ What kind of food do they serve?

_1_ How about dinner next Friday?

_____ How big is it?

_____ What about Carlito's?

_____ Which restaurant do you want to go to?

2 **Group Work** Read the How To box. In groups of four, suggest local restaurants for tonight.

> ### How To:
> #### Make suggestions
> | | |
> |---|---|
> | *What about dinner next week?* | *Good idea!/Yes./OK.* |
> | *How about Luciano's Restaurant?* | *No, I don't like that restaurant.* |

Grammar | question words

3 Match the questions in the Active Grammar box to the answers below.

_____ a. He likes all kinds of food.

_____ b. It's near my house.

_____ c. She's a chef.

_____ d. It's very big.

_____ e. I like the new one.

_____ f. He's my friend.

4 Complete the sentences with question words from the Active Grammar box.

1. ___How___ rich is she?

2. _____ fruit do you like?

3. _____ do you live?

4. _____ is your boss?

5. _____ 's your name?

6. _____ sofa do you like—this one or that one?

Active Grammar

Where	1. *Where is Carlito's?*
Who	2. *Who is he?*
What	3. *What does she do?*
What kind of + noun	4. *What kind of food does he like?*
Which + noun	5. *Which restaurant do you like—the new one or the old one?*
How + adjective	6. *How big is it?*

See Reference page 88

> ### How To:
> #### Reserve a table at a restaurant
> | | |
> |---|---|
> | **Customer:** | *I'd like to reserve a table for Friday afternoon/Saturday night.* |
> | **Waiter:** | *How many people?* |
> | | *What time?* |
> | | *What's the name, please?* |

Speaking

5 **Pair Work** Read the How To box. Make reservations.

Student A: Call Carlito's restaurant. Reserve a table for Saturday evening.

Student B: You work at Carlito's restaurant. Answer the phone.

Vocabulary | food

6a Match the <u>underlined</u> words in the menu to the pictures.

1. _chicken_   6. _____

2. _____   7. _____

3. _____   8. _____

4. _____   9. _____

5. _____   10. _____

b ▶2.28 Listen and check your answers.

c **Pair Work** Say what food you like or don't like from the menu.

d **Group Work** Choose your favorite appetizer, main course, and dessert from the menu. Tell the group.

> *I'd like the fish soup, the lamb chops for the main course, and the ice cream for dessert.*

7a ▶2.29 Listen. What do Mark and Anna choose from the menu?

b **Group Work** Work in groups of three. Look at Audioscript 2.29 on page 127. Read the conversation aloud but change the food.

> *Are you ready to order?*

> *Yes. I'd like a house salad, please.*

Menu

CARLITO'S

APPETIZERS

Seafood cocktail
<u>Fish</u> soup
House salad

MAIN COURSES

Roast <u>beef</u> *
Roast <u>chicken</u>*
<u>Lamb</u> chops *
Vegetable <u>pasta</u>
* with <u>potatoes</u> or <u>rice</u>

DESSERTS

Ice cream
<u>Chocolate</u> cake
<u>Cheese</u> and fruit

Speaking

8 **SPEAKING EXCHANGE** Work in groups of three.

Student A: You are the waiter at Salt and Pepper restaurant.

Students B and C: You are customers at Salt and Pepper restaurant. Look at the menu on page 114. Enter the restaurant and order your meal.

> *Good evening. Do you have a reservation?*

> *Yes, we do. My name is . . .*

Review

1 Complete the conversation with the correct form of the words in parentheses. Then practice with a partner.

A: Do you want ___*to go*___ (1. go) to a movie this afternoon?

B: There's a good movie on TV. Do you want _____ (2. watch) TV?

A: I don't like _____ (3. watch) TV.

B: OK. Well, I like _____ (4. swim), and it's hot today. Do you want _____ (5. go) swimming?

A: I can't swim. Do you want _____ (6. go) sightseeing?

B: Yes. I want _____ (7. take) some photos with my new camera.

2 Complete the email with the correct form of *have*.

3 Write questions and answers using *have* and the words in parentheses. Then practice with a partner.

1. A: ___*Does your sister have a dishwasher*___ ?
   (your sister/dishwasher)

   B: ___*Yes, she does*___ . (Yes)

2. A: _____ ?
   (you/car)

   B: _____ . (No)

3. A: _____ ?
   (your parents/TV)

   B: _____ . (No)

4. A: _____ ?
   (James/bicycle)

   B: _____ . (Yes)

5. A: _____ ?
   (they/new email address)

   B: _____ . (No)

6. A: _____ ?
   (she/good dictionary)

   B: _____ . (Yes)

Hi Benita,

Thanks for your email. Please come to my house when you visit Vancouver. ___*I have*___ (1. I/✓) a guest bedroom, so you can stay there. _____ (2. it/✓) a big bed and an armchair. _____ (3. it/✗) a television, but _____ (4. it/✓) a bathroom. Can you drive? _____ (5. I/✗) a car, but _____ (6. my parents/✓) one. _____ (7. you) a bicycle? _____ (8. My husband/✓) one, and you can use it.

See you next week!

Love,

Amy

4 Write a question for each answer. Use *what*, *where*, *who*, *how*, *which*, or *what kind of*. Then practice with a partner.

1. A: ___*What do you do*___ ?
   B: I'm a teacher.

2. A: _____ ?
   B: She's not very tall.

3. A: _____ ?
   B: I like Italian food and Chinese food.

4. A: _____ ?
   B: I like this coffee table. That coffee table is small.

5. A: _____ ?
   B: I live in Quito in Ecuador.

6. A: _____ ?
   B: She's my friend.

Communication | ask for and give information about people

5 **Pair Work** Look at the people and their apartments. What does each person like doing? Tell your partner.

> 9c: He likes playing golf.

> 9b: She likes to watch sports.

6 **Pair Work** Complete four of the addresses below. Don't show your partner.

Student A: Look at page 111 in the Speaking Exchange.
Student B: Look at page 114 in the Speaking Exchange.

Mr. O. Pamuk 7 Oak Lane _____	Ms. A. Walker 7 Oak Lane _____	Mr. S. Kato 7 Oak Lane _____	Ms. T. Morrison 7 Oak Lane _____	Mr. J. Heller 7 Oak Lane _____
Ms. Z. Smith 7 Oak Lane _____	Mr. J. Coe 7 Oak Lane _____	Mr. M. Haddon 7 Oak Lane _____	Ms. M. Atwood 7 Oak Lane _____	Mrs. A. Garcia 7 Oak Lane _____

7 **Pair Work** Ask your partner *Yes/No* questions with *like* to complete the other four addresses.

> Does Mr. Coe like reading?

> No, he doesn't. Does Ms. Walker . . .

Unit 8 Reference

like + gerund/infinitive; *want* + infinitive

When a verb follows *like*, it is in the gerund form (*-ing*) or the infinitive form (*to* + verb).

   *I like **reading**.*   *I like **to read**.*

When a verb follows *want*, it is always in the infinitive form (*to* + verb).

   *I want **to read**.*

have

Have is an irregular verb.

I You We They	➕ ➖	have don't have	a bicycle. a televison. a brother. two sisters.
He She It	➕ ➖	has doesn't have	
❓ Do	I/you/we/they	have	any cousins?
❓ Does	he/she/it		a cat?

Yes, I/you/we/they do.
Yes, he/she/it does.
No, I/you/we/they don't.
No, he/she/it doesn't.

Question words

- Use *where* for places.
  ***Where** are you from?*
  ***Where** do you live?*
- Use *who* for people.
  ***Who** are you?*
  ***Who** do you play tennis with?*

You can also use *who* to ask about the company someone works for.

   ***Who** do you work for?*

- Use *what* for things.
  ***What**'s your name?*
  ***What** do you do?*

- Use *what kind of* + noun for types.
  ***What kind of** ice cream is there?*
  ***What kind of** books do you have?*
- Use *which* for things when there is a choice.
  ***Which** dictionary do you have?*
  ***Which** John Lennon song is your favorite?*
- Use *how* + adjective for amounts.
  ***How** tall is he?*
  ***How** old are you?*
- Note these questions:
  How much is it? (price)
  How many cars do you have? (quantity)
  How often do you go out? (frequency)

Make suggestions

Use *What about . . . ?* or *How about . . .?* + noun to make suggestions.

   ***What about** the new restaurant on Clark Street?*
   ***How about** a week at the beach this summer?*

Unit Vocabulary

Leisure activities

go biking	go sightseeing	play soccer
go hiking	go out to eat	work out
play tennis	read a book	
watch TV	go swimming	
play chess	go to the theater	

Adjectives

boring	exciting	fun
easy	difficult	interesting

Rooms and furniture

living room:	sofa	coffee table	
	lamp	armchair	
bedroom:	bed	window	wardrobe
kitchen:	sink	fridge	dishwasher
	stove	cabinet	
bathroom:	sink	mirror	
	toilet	bathtub	
garage:	car	bicycle	

Food

fish	lamb	potatoes	chocolate
rice	pasta	seafood	
beef	cheese	chicken	

UNIT 9
Your life

A Beijing Summer Olympics

B Wall Street Crash

C Fall of the Berlin Wall

D Mandela: New President of South Africa

Warm Up

1 Look at the photos. Match each photo to a year. _____ 1989 _____ 1994 _____ 2008 _____ 1929

2a Match a year in the box to a headline below. (1963 1946 2011 1977 2004 1912 2002 2010)

_____ a. First iPod in Stores

_____ b. William and Kate Royal Wedding

_____ c. Tsunami in Southeast Asia

_____ d. Titanic Disaster

_____ e. Martin Luther King: "I have a dream"

_____ f. Haiti Earthquake

_____ g. Juan Peron: President of Argentina

_____ h. Elvis Presley Is Dead

b **Pair Work** Tell your partner what you think.

c ▶2.30 Listen and check your answers.

> I think "First iPod in Stores" is 2004.

> I think it's 2002.

Make simple statements about people from history

GRAMMAR simple past of *be:* affirmative statements

| A | Michael Jackson | | B | Princess Diana | | C | Elvis Presley | | D | Bruce Lee |

Reading

1a Read the biographies. Match a biography to a photo.

He was a singer and an actor. He was born on January 8, 1935. His parents were very poor. He was a factory worker and then a truck driver. His first song was "That's All Right." He was "The King of Rock and Roll."

_____ 1.

He was an actor and fighter. He was born on November 27, 1940, in San Francisco. His parents were from Hong Kong. They weren't rich. His father was a singer. His last movie was *Enter the Dragon.* He was short and thin, but he was very strong and fast.

_____ 3.

He was a singer and dancer. He was born on August 29, 1958. He was the lead singer of a group at the age of 11. His album *Thriller* was the top album of all time. He was "The King of Pop."

_____ 2.

She was a princess and a fashion icon. She was born on July 1, 1961. Her parents were rich. She wasn't a good student at school, but she was a good pianist. Her husband was Prince Charles. Their life together was not happy.

_____ 4.

b Complete the sentences with names from the photos.

1. _Michael Jackson_ and _Elvis Presley_ were singers.
2. _____ and _____ were actors.
3. _____ and _____ were poor as children.
4. _____ was rich.

c **Pair Work** Close your books. What can you remember about the people in the paragraphs in Exercise 1a?

> *Bruce Lee was born in San Francisco. His parents were . . .*

Grammar | simple past of *be*: affirmative statements

2a Complete the Active Grammar box with *was* or *were*.

b ▶ 2.31 Listen and check your answers.

3 Complete the sentences with *was* or *were*.

1. Coco Chanel __was__ a fashion designer.
2. Picasso and Matisse _____ famous for their paintings.
3. Colonel Tom Parker _____ Elvis Presley's manager.
4. Jackie Chan and Oprah Winfrey _____ born in 1954.
5. We _____ good soccer players in 1990. We don't play soccer now.
6. I _____ a good pianist at school.

4a Read the How To box. Then write two true sentences and one false sentence about you and your family.

b **Pair Work** Read your sentences to your partner. Your partner guesses true or false.

> When my father was young, he was an actor.   False.   No, it's true!

Active Grammar

I	was	an actor.
You	were	a singer.
He	_____	happy.
She	_____	born in 1982.
It	_____	great.
We	were	singers.
They	_____	rich.

See Reference page 98

How To:

Talk about childhood

When I was a child, I was a good singer.
When they were young, they were very poor.

Vocabulary | collocations with prepositions

5a Complete the biographies with prepositions from the box.

> on   for   with   ~~in~~   of   at

She was <u>born</u> __in__ (1.) 1929 in New York. She was <u>good</u> _____ (2.) horseback-riding and painting. Her husbands were John F. Kennedy, the <u>president</u> _____ (3.) the US, and then Aristotle Onassis, a Greek businessman.

Billie Holiday was <u>born</u> _____ (4.) April 7, 1915, in Philadelphia. She was <u>famous</u> _____ (5.) her music. She was <u>friends</u> _____ (6.) the jazz musician Lester Young. Her husbands were bad men and she was unhappy.

b **Pair Work** Say an underlined word from the paragraphs above. Your partner says the preposition.

> good   good at

6a Who is your favorite person from the 20th century? Write notes about him or her.

b **Pair Work** Tell your partner about this person. Your partner guesses the person.

> He was born in the UK. He was a singer and songwriter.

Give a short description of a past experience

GRAMMAR simple past of *be*: negatives and questions

Poker

Scrabble

Mahjong

Speaking

1 **Pair Work** Talk about the games. Use the phrases below.

> I know how to play . . .

> I don't know how to play . . .

> It's difficult/easy/boring/exciting/fun/interesting.

Listening

2a ▶2.32 Listen to Kenji, Isabella, and Mei Ling playing a game called *my first, my last*. In the game you can't answer questions with *yes* or *no*. What does Isabella talk about?

b Listen again. Circle the correct words about Kenji and Mei Ling below.

KENJI'S FIRST TEACHER

1. Her name was *Miss*/*Mrs.* Lloyd.
2. She was about *50*/*60* years old.
3. She was a *good*/*bad* teacher.
4. Her favorite student was *Koji*/*Kenji*.

MEI LING'S LAST VACATION

1. Mei Ling's last vacation was *two*/*three* years ago.
2. It was to a *Pacific*/*Caribbean* island.
3. Mei Ling was with *her parents*/*a friend*.
4. There were *mountains*/*beaches* on the island.

Grammar | simple past of *be*: negatives and questions

3 Look at Audioscript 2.32 on page 128 and complete the Active Grammar box with *was*, *wasn't*, or *were*.

Active Grammar

⊖			?		
I _____ (was not)	a good student.		Was I	a good student?	
You weren't	happy at school.		_____ you	happy at school?	
He/She/It _____	interesting.		_____ he/she/it	interesting?	
We weren't	good students.		Were we	good students?	
They weren't	in my class.		Were they	in my class?	

?		
What was her name?	Who was your favorite teacher?	
Where were your books?	When was your class?	

See Reference page 98

Chess

Monopoly

4 Complete the sentences with *was, wasn't, were,* or *weren't.*

1. I __was__ very quiet at school. (✓)
2. My first car _____ very big, but it was fun. (✗)
3. Who _____ your friends at school?
4. What _____ your favorite subject at school?
5. You _____ at school. (✗)
6. _____ you late this morning?

Pronunciation | sentence stress

5 ▶2·33 Listen. Mark the stress.

1. I was a <u>good</u> <u>stu</u>dent.
2. He wasn't very intelligent.
3. They weren't very happy.
4. Was she a good teacher?
5. Who were your friends?

Vocabulary | time expressions: *yesterday, last, ago*

6 Complete the time expressions with *yesterday, ago,* or *last.*

1. today
2. yesterday
3. _____ night
4. _____ morning
5. two days _____
6. _____ week
7. _____ month
8. six months _____
9. _____ year
10. ten years _____

Speaking

7a **Pair Work** When were these past experiences? Tell your partner.

- your first day at school
- your last meal in a restaurant
- your first vacation
- your last flight
- your first job
- your first email

My first day at school was 22 years ago.

b **Pair Work** Ask your partner questions with *Where were you . . . ?* and a time expression.

Where were you yesterday afternoon?

I was at home.

8 **SPEAKING EXCHANGE** Work in groups of three or four. Play *my first, my last* on page 115.

Writing

9 Write a paragraph about your first teacher or your last vacation. You can start like this:

My first teacher was . . . She/He was . . .
My last vacation was (six months) ago . . . It was to . . .

Make a simple request and ask permission

GRAMMAR *can/could I:* permission; *can/could you:* requests

Vocabulary | housework

1a Match a picture below to a phrase in the box.

> _____ do the laundry _____ vacuum the house _____ cook dinner
>
> _____ clean the bathroom _____ wash the dishes _____ iron a shirt

1 2 3 4  5  6

b ▶ 2·34 Listen and check your answers.

2 **Pair Work** Who does these things in your house? Tell your partner.

> *My wife does the laundry.*   *I iron my shirts.*

Reading

3a Read the article.

Who does the housework now?

In the 1950s, life was simple. Women were housewives and men were factory workers, managers, sales reps, sales assistants, etc. But in the 21st century, life is different. Now, there are over 140,000 househusbands in the US. They stay at home and look after the children. We talk to one househusband, Jeff Timberland.

Do you like your job as a househusband?
Jeff: Yes, I do. Plus, childcare is $250 for one week, for one child. It's very expensive.

What does your wife do?
Jeff: She's an architect.

Do you like doing housework?
Jeff: I don't like ironing—it's very boring. And I don't like washing the dishes. But I like vacuuming the house and cooking dinner.

What was your job before?
Jeff: I was a sales rep. I was a good sales rep, and I was happy. But my children are my job now.

Do you want to get another job?
Jeff: Yes, but not now. My kids are very young. They want their dad, not a stranger.

b **Pair Work** Take turns asking and answering the questions below.

1. How many househusbands are there in the US now?
2. Does Jeff like his job as a househusband?
3. What is Jeff's wife's occupation?
4. What housework does Jeff like doing?
5. What did Jeff do before?
6. Does Jeff want to get a new job now?

c **Group Work** Work in small groups. Discuss.

1. Are there a lot of househusbands in your country?
2. Who usually looks after young children in your country?
3. Jeff says, "They want their dad, not a stranger." Do you agree?

Listening

4a ▶2.35 Listen to four events in Jeff's week. Match each conversation to its picture.

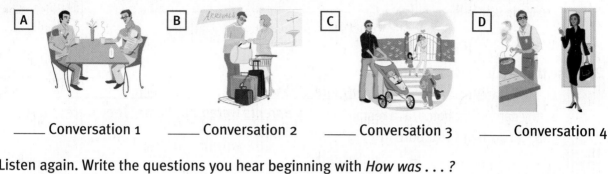

_____ Conversation 1   _____ Conversation 2   _____ Conversation 3   _____ Conversation 4

b Listen again. Write the questions you hear beginning with *How was . . . ?*

1. How was _____ ?
2. How was _____ ?
3. How was _____ ?
4. How was _____ ?

5 **Group Work** Read the How To box. Work in small groups. Ask questions with *How was . . . ?*

> How was your weekend?

> It was fine, thanks. I went to a concert on Sunday

How To:

Ask about an experience

How was	your weekend?/your week?/ your day?/your flight?
It was great. 🙂	It was OK. 🙂
It wasn't very good. 🙁	It was awful. 😠

Grammar | *Can/Could I . . . ?; Can/Could you . . . ?*

6 Complete the Active Grammar box with *I* or *you*.

Speaking

7 **Pair Work** Use the cues to ask your partner questions.

- use your pen
- spell your name
- use your cell phone
- give me your email address
- give me some money
- open the window
- look at your book

> Could I use your pen?

> Yes, of course.

Active Grammar

Can	_____	use your telephone?
Could		have a cup of coffee?
Yes, _____ can.		No, I'm sorry.
Can	_____	carry my bags?
Could		iron my shirt?
Yes, of course.		I'm sorry, I can't.

See Reference page 98

Review

1 Complete the paragraph with *was* or *were* and guess the famous person.

> Who am I?
>
> I am a singer with a very famous band. I _**was**_ (1.) born on July 26, 1943, in the UK. My father and my grandfather _____ (2.) teachers. My mother _____ (3.) from Australia. I _____ (4.) a student at the London School of Economics—but only for two years. Jerry Hall and Bianca Moreno de Macias _____ (5.) my wives. "Paint It Black" and "Satisfaction" _____ (6.) two of my band's famous songs.

2 Use the words to write sentences.

1. Sally/late/early   *Sally wasn't late. She was early.*_____

2. My parents/at home/at a restaurant   *My parents weren't at home. They were at a restaurant.*

3. Rick/born in 1981/born in 1979
   _____

4. It/a good movie/very boring
   _____

5. We/rich/very poor
   _____

6. Kerry and Mark/in Bogotá/in Cali
   _____

3 Use the words to write questions. Match the questions with the answers below. Then ask and answer them with a partner.

1. born?/When/you/were   _*When were you born?*___ = _e_

2. was/Who/manager?/your   _____ = ___

3. school?/your/Where/was   _____ = ___

4. first/What/your/job?/was   _____ = ___

5. weekend?/your/was/How   _____ = ___

| a. I was a factory worker. | c. Her name was Ms. Dickson. | e. In 1990. |
| b. It was great, thanks. | d. It was on Peak Street, near the hospital. | |

4 Circle the correct word to complete each sentence.

1. Can *I/you* tell me the time?
2. Could *I/you* open the door?
3. Can *I/you* help you?
4. Can *I/you* tell me your name, please?
5. Could *I/you* pass me the salt, please?
6. Could *I/you* listen to your new CD?

5 Circle the correct word to complete each sentence.

1. Where were you *yesterday/last/ago* night?
2. Who usually *vacuums/cleans/does* the laundry?
3. I was in Colombia six months *yesterday/last/ago*.
4. What was she famous *on/to/for*?
5. Where were you *yesterday/last/ago* afternoon?
6. Can you *wash/vacuum/iron* the house today?
7. He's friends *of/with/to* Mark Heller.
8. Are you good *on/to/at* tennis?

Communication | talk about school days

6 ▶2.36 Match a subject in the box to a picture. Then listen and repeat.

_____ math _____ languages _____ science _____ music _____ art _____ sports

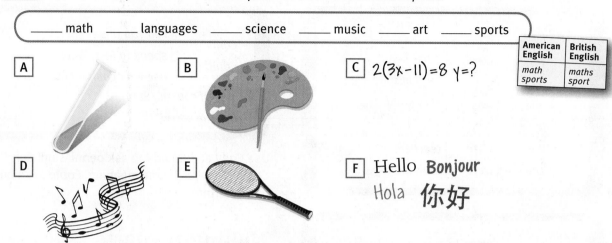

	American English	British English
	math	maths
	sports	sport

A

B

C $2(3x-11)=8$ $y=?$

D

E

F Hello **Bonjour**
Hola 你好

7a ▶2.37 Listen and complete the form for Louise.

b Listen again. Check your answers.

8a Complete the form in Exercise 7a so that it is true for you.

b **Pair Work** Make sentences based on the chart. Tell your partner.

> I was very good at math.

> Really? I wasn't. I was good at music.

My school days

School name:
Washington High School

Where: _____

Years: _____

Good/bad school

Good at: _____

Bad at: _____

Favorite class: _____

Best friend: _____

Good/bad student

9 **Group Work** Close your books and ask other students about their school days.

> What was the name of your high school?

> Were you a good student?

Unit 9 Reference

Simple past of *be*

⊕	I	was	
	You	were	a teacher.
	He		born in 1983.
	She	was	very good.
	It		
	We	were	teachers.
	They	were	born in 1983.

⊖	I	wasn't (was not)	
	You	weren't (were not)	a teacher. born in 1983.
	He		very good.
	She	wasn't (was not)	
	It		
	We	weren't (were not)	teachers.
	They	weren't (were not)	born in 1983.

?	Was	I	
	Were	you	a teacher?
		he	born in 1983?
	Was	she	very good?
		it	
	Were	we	teachers?
	Were	they	born in 1983?

?	
Who was your manager?
What were their names?
Where was your school?
Which store was your favorite?
When was the interview?
How old were you in 2000?

Asking permission

Can I	call you this evening?
Could I	speak to Mrs. Walsh?
	use your computer?
Yes, of course./Sure.	
No, I'm sorry.	

Use *Can I* and *Could I* to ask permission. *Can I* and *Could I* have the same meaning. *Could I* is a bit more polite/formal.

Making requests

Can you	call me this evening?
Could you	answer the phone?
Yes, of course./Sure.	
No, I'm sorry.	

Use *Can you* and *Could you* to make a request. *Can you* and *Could you* have the same meaning, but *Could you* is a bit more polite or formal.

Time expressions

Yesterday
yesterday   yesterday evening   yesterday afternoon
yesterday morning

Last
last night   last week   last month   last year

Ago
five months ago   eight years ago   two days ago
a week ago

Unit Vocabulary

Adjectives and prepositions
born in (Paris)   born on (October 3rd)
bad at (soccer)   famous for (his books)
friends with (Madonna)
good at (tennis/dancing)
the president of the United States

Housework
do the laundry   vacuum the house
cook dinner   clean the bathroom
iron a shirt   wash the dishes

UNIT 10
Past and future events

A

B

C

D

Warm Up

1a Complete each sentence with a verb from the box.

> win   arrests   get   meet   ~~lose~~   steals   find   break   stay   move

1. You _lose_____ your wallet.
2. A thief _____ your cell phone.
3. You _____ in bed all day.
4. You _____ the lottery.
5. You _____ married.

6. You _____ $10 on the street.
7. A police officer _____ you.
8. You _____ to a new house.
9. You _____ your leg.
10. You _____ your favorite actor.

b ▶2.38 Listen and check your answers.

c Look at the photos. Match each picture to a sentence in Exercise 1a.

LESSON 1
Understand a simple narrative of past events
GRAMMAR simple past: regular verbs

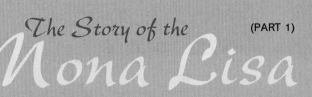

The Story of the Mona Lisa (PART 1)

Every day, 15,000 people visit the Louvre museum in Paris. Most of them want to see the "Mona Lisa." But what is the story of this painting?

The artist was, of course, Leonardo da Vinci. He started the painting in 1503, and he finished it about four years later. Leonardo was Italian, but in 1516 he moved to France with the painting. The King of France liked it, and the "Mona Lisa" stayed in France.

Reading

1   Read "The Story of the Mona Lisa (Part 1)" aloud. Complete the information below.

Place (now): _The Louvre, Paris_   Finished painting: _____

Artist: _____ Moved to France: _____

Started painting: _____

Grammar | simple past affirmative: regular verbs

2a   Underline the verbs in "The Story of the Mona Lisa (Part 1)."

b   Which verbs are in the simple past?

c   How do you make the simple past of regular verbs?

3   Complete the Active Grammar box with the correct form of the verb.

4   Complete each paragraph with verbs from each box in the simple past.

Active Grammar

simple present	simple past
I like the painting.	I liked the painting.
She stays with her friends.	She _____ with her friends.

See Reference page 108

(finish   ~~want~~   start   ask)

Pope Julius II _wanted_ (1.) a new ceiling in the Sistine Chapel. He _____ (2.) Michelangelo to paint the ceiling of the Sistine Chapel. Michelangelo _____ (3.) it in 1508. He _____ (4.) it in 1512.

(live   work   play   move (x2))

Marcel Duchamp was an artist. He was born in 1887. He _____ (5.) in Paris, and he _____ (6.) chess with his brothers. In 1914, he _____ (7.) to New York. He _____ (8.) in a library in New York. In 1918, he _____ (9.) to Argentina.

Pronunciation | simple past -ed endings

5a ▶2.39 Listen and repeat the simple past form of the verbs in the box.

> wanted ____ asked ____ moved ____ started ____ finished ____ lived ____ played ____
>
> worked ____ talked ____ closed ____ cooked ____ arrested ____ walked ____ listened ____

b How do you pronounce the -ed ending of each verb? Write *t*, *d*, or *id* next to each verb in the box.

c ▶2.40 Listen and check your answers. Then repeat.

Listening

6 ▶2.41 Listen to "The Story of the Mona Lisa (Part 2)." Mark the sentences true (*T*) or false (*F*).

_____ a. The "Mona Lisa" moved to the Louvre.　_____ d. The police talked to Picasso.

_____ b. It stayed in Napoleon's bedroom.　_____ e. The police talked to Vincenzo Peruggia.

_____ c. The Louvre closed in 1910.

Grammar | simple past: negatives and questions

7 Complete the Active Grammar box with *did* or *didn't*.

Active Grammar

⊖	I/You/He/She/ It/We/They	didn't stay	in Italy.	
		_____ talk	to the police.	
❓	_____	I/you/he/she/it/ we/they	stay	in Italy?	Yes, I/you/he/she/it/we/they _____ .
			talk	to the police?	No, I/you/he/she/it/we/they _____ .

See Reference page 108

8a Use the words to write negative sentences.

1. Picasso/not like/the "Mona Lisa"　　*Picasso didn't like the "Mona Lisa."*
2. Leonardo da Vinci/not live/Spain　　_____
3. the "Mona Lisa"/not stay/Italy　　_____

b Use the words to write questions and answers.

1. the police/arrest/Picasso?　A: *Did the police arrest Picasso*?　B: No, *they didn't* .
2. Andy Warhol/work for/*Vogue*?　A: _____? B: Yes, _____.
3. Van Gogh/move to/London?　A: _____? B: Yes, _____.

Speaking

9 **SPEAKING EXCHANGE** Read the last part of the story on page 114. Ask and answer the questions.

1. Who was the thief?　　　　　　　3. How did the thief steal the "Mona Lisa"?
2. Where was the "Mona Lisa" for two years?

Give a simple summary of a news event ✓ CAN DO

GRAMMAR simple past: irregular verbs

Reading

1a Read the magazine page. Fill in the blanks in each story with *good* or *bad*.

Good Week, Bad Week

MONDAY JUNE 12

3. It was a _____ week for pop group Gilt. Gilt's concert was last Friday, but the tickets said "Saturday." "Only five people came and saw the concert," said Sia Kahn, Gilt's singer. "They took photos and bought a T-shirt, but it wasn't a good day."

1. It was a _____ week for actor Romero Cline, age 43. He went to Las Vegas last week and he met Monica Hawkins, a waitress in a fast food restaurant. Three days later, they got married.

2. It was a _____ week for Mr. and Mrs. Blatt from the US. They had fish for dinner, and they found three gold coins inside the fish. "The fish was $3.50," said Mrs. Blatt, "but the gold coins are worth $1,000 each!"

CROSSWORD*

*(See page 103, Exercise 4)

4. It was a _____ week for Emiliana Rotman from Sweden. She won €14 million in the Euro lottery, but she lost her ticket. "Never mind," said Emiliana, "That's life!"

b ▶2.42 Listen and check your answers.

c Mark these statements true (*T*) or false (*F*).

_T_ **1.** Romero Cline got married last week.

_____ **2.** Monica Hawkins works in a restaurant.

_____ **3.** Emiliana Rotman doesn't have €14 million.

_____ **4.** Emiliana Rotman is very sad.

_____ **5.** Gilt's concert was on Saturday.

_____ **6.** Sia Kahn bought a T-shirt.

_____ **7.** The Blatts found coins under the fish.

_____ **8.** Mr. and Mrs. Blatt bought three fish.

2 **Pair Work** Close your books. What can you remember about the four stories?

Grammar | simple past: irregular verbs

3a Look at the magazine page in Exercise 1a on page 102 again. <u>Underline</u> all the verbs in the simple past.

b Complete the Active Grammar box with *take* or *took*.

4 Complete the crossword on page 102 with the simple past form of the regular and irregular verbs below.

> **ACROSS**
> 3 come   5 play   8 see   9 buy
> 12 finish   14 have   15 move   16 go
> **DOWN**
> 1 meet   2 ask   4 listen   6 get
> 7 win   10 find   11 say   13 lose

5 **Pair Work** Look at the phrases in the box. Which did or didn't you do last week? Tell your partner.

> go to a supermarket   lose something
> have fish for dinner   find money
> come to class late   take a photo
> buy new clothes   see a concert

Active Grammar

➕	I/You/He She/We/They	**went** to Paris.
		_____ photos.
➖	I/You/He/ She/We/They	**didn't go** to Paris.
		didn't _____ photos.
❓	**Did**	I/you/he/ she/we/ they	**go** to Paris?
			_____ photos?
	Yes, I/you/he/she/we/they **did**.	
	No, I/you/he/she/we/they **didn't**.	

See Reference page 108

Speaking

6a **Group Work** Ask five people, "How was last week for you?" Ask why.

b **Pair Work** Tell a new partner about the people you talked to.

> *It was a good week for Pedro. He started a new job, and he went to a concert.*

Vocabulary | large numbers

7a Read the How To box. When is *and* used?

> **How To:**
>
> | **Say large numbers** | |
> |---|---|
> | 100 | *a hundred/one hundred* |
> | 915 | *nine hundred and fifteen* |
> | 1,000 | *a thousand/one thousand* |
> | 2,690 | *two thousand six hundred and ninety* |

b ▶2·43 Listen and write the prices in the ad.

8 **Pair Work** Now tell your partner the prices.

> *The DVD player was $199. Now it's $149.*

Writing

9 Write a short good week/bad week news story.

was _$199_
sale price
_$149_

was $_____
sale price
$_____

was $_____
sale price
$_____

was $_____
sale price
$_____

was $_____
sale price
$_____

was $_____
sale price
$_____

Abby
Charlie
Haley
Nick

Listening

1   **Pair Work** Ask and answer the questions below.

    1. How was your week?   **2.** What happened in the last seven days?

2a ▶2.44 Listen and match a person in the photo to their week below. Write the names.

    1. an exciting week   **2.** an interesting week   **3.** busy week (x2)

    _____   _____   _____ _____

  b Listen again. Complete the chart below with notes.

	What happened?	What are his or her plans?
Nick	*talked to manager*	*find a new job*
Abby		
Charlie		
Haley		

Grammar | *be going to*

3   Complete the Active Grammar box with *'s*, *is*, *not,* and *are*. Look at Audioscript 2.44 on page 128 to help you.

Active Grammar

⊕	I'm	going to	get married.
	She _____		find a new job.
⊖	He's	not going to	move to Texas.
	They're	_____ going to	get married soon.
?	_____ you	going to	have a party?
	_____ she		see Daniel tonight?
?	What _____ you	going to	do tomorrow?
	Where _____ he		stay?

See Reference page 108

4a Look at Nick, Haley, and Charlie's plans for tomorrow. Write complete sentences.

	Nick	Haley and Charlie
tomorrow	~~play football~~ play tennis	~~eat out~~ stay at home
next Sunday	~~write a report~~ stay in bed all day	~~go for a walk~~ have lunch with friends
next Monday	~~work from home~~ visit a customer	~~work~~ take a day off

> Nick's not going to play football tomorrow.
> He's going to play tennis.

b **Pair Work** Ask questions from the chart above.

c **Pair Work** Tell your partner your plans for next week.

Vocabulary | future plans

5a Match each phrase in the box to a photo.

> _____ get in shape   _____ retire   _____ start a business
> _____ learn to drive   _____ go to college   _____ have a child/children

b **Pair Work** Which of the phrases did you, your friends, or your family do in the past? Which of these things are you going to do in the future? Tell your partner.

Speaking

6 **Pair Work** Imagine you win $3 million in the lottery. What are you going to do? Make notes and then tell your partner.

Review

1 Complete the email with the simple past form of the verbs in the box.

> watch   talk   cook   ~~work~~   visit   stay   play

> Hi Felicia,
>
> How was your weekend? I _worked_ (1.) on Saturday ☺ — I have a lot of work at the moment. In the evening, my friend _____ (2.) dinner for me and we _____ (3.) a movie. That was nice! On Sunday morning, I _____ (4.) tennis with my friends, and in the afternoon, my cousin _____ (5.) me. He lives in Taipei. We _____ (6.) at home and _____ (7.) about our lives. He's very happy in Taipei.
>
> Hope you're OK. Send me an email soon!
>
> Kayo

2 Use the words to write complete sentences in the simple past.

1. My friend/start/a new job
   My friend started a new job .

2. Julio/move/to America?
   _____ ?

3. I/not talk/to my boss
   _____ .

4. you/play chess/with Michelle?
   _____ ?

5. Mei and I/cook/dinner
   _____ .

6. Paul/not like/his present
   _____ .

3 **Pair Work** Work with a partner. Find the simple past form of the verbs below in the word grid.

1. have   3. take   5. give   7. go
2. find   4. meet   6. steal   8. say

e	y	u	b	f	l
m	e	t	o	o	k
s	a	i	d	u	k
t	a	z	g	n	m
o	g	h	a	d	v
l	j	f	v	d	f
e	s	w	e	n	t

4 Complete each sentence with the simple past form of the verb in parentheses.

1. How _did_ you _break_ your arm? (break)
2. They _____ a lot of money. (win)
3. Why _____ the police _____ them? (arrest)
4. Your mother _____ to the supermarket. (go)

5 Write questions to find the missing information. Then practice with a partner. Make up answers.

1. __?__'s going to retire.
   Who's going to retire ?

2. I'm going to buy a __?__.
   What are you going to buy ?

3. They're going to __?__.
   _____ ?

4. I'm going to call __?__.
   _____ ?

5. Lucy's going to go to __?__ University.
   _____ ?

6. Tom and Minnie are going to move to __?__.
   _____ ?

Communication | talk about past and future vacations

6a Think about your favorite vacation from your past. Answer the questions.

1. When was it? _____
2. Where did you go? _____
3. Who did you go with? _____
4. How long did you stay? _____
5. Where did you stay (hotel, B&B, etc.)? _____
6. What did you do? _____

b **Pair Work** Use your notes to tell your partner about your vacation.

> *My favorite vacation was in 2010. I went to South Africa with my wife, and we went on a safari. We stayed for two weeks and . . .*

7a **Pair Work** What places are in the photos? Which places would you like to visit? What other places would you really like to visit?

b Imagine you and your partner win a vacation of a lifetime. Read the rules.

c **Pair Work** Plan your vacation. Choose three destinations and make notes on:

1. where (**Ex:** Beijing, China)
2. how long (**Ex:** four days)
3. plans (**Ex:** eat Chinese food, see the palace)

The Rules

1 It is a two-week vacation.
2 You can fly to three different places.
3 You always travel together.

> *How about Beijing?*   *Yes, good idea. I want to go there. How long are we going to stay?*

8 **Pair Work** Find a new partner. Explain your vacation plans to your new partner.

> *First, we're going to fly to Beijing, China. We're going to stay there for four days. We're going to see the Forbidden City and we're going to eat Chinese food. Then we're going to fly to . . .*

Unit 10 Reference

Simple past

Regular verbs

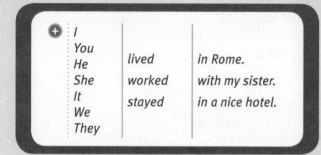

To make the simple past of regular verbs, add -ed or -d to the end of the verb.

Irregular verbs

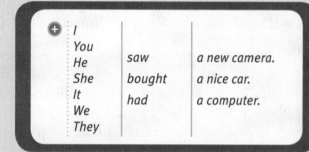

A lot of verbs are irregular in the simple past affirmative; for example:

buy—bought	come—came	do—did
eat—ate	find—found	get—got
give—gave	go—went	have—had
make—made	read /rid/—read /rɛd/	
say—said	see—saw	speak—spoke
win—won	write—wrote	

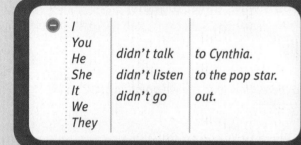

Use *didn't* + verb to make the negative. Do not use the past form in the negative.

~~She didn't went to the concert.~~

She didn't go to the concert.

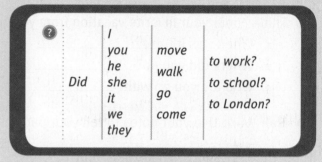

Use *Did* + subject + verb to make questions. Do not use the past form in the question.

~~Did they moved to Paris?~~

Did they move to Paris?

be going to

Use *going to* + verb to talk about plans for the future.

I	'm		
You	're		
He		going to	get in shape.
She	's	not going to	retire.
It			get married.
We	're		
They	're		
Am	I		
Are	you		
Is	he she it	going to	take the bus? visit my sister?
Are	we		
Are	they		

Unit Vocabulary

Verbs + nouns

steal a cell phone	lose your wallet
break your arm	win the lottery
move to a new house	find money
meet a famous person	stay in bed

Future plans

get in shape	learn to drive
go to college	have a child/children
start a new business	retire

Speaking Exchange

Unit 2 | Page 23, Exercise 5a

You are Terri.

Name: Terri Nielson

Age: 28

From: New York

Address: 19 Filmore Street

Cell No: 917-555-0109

You are Victoria.

Name: Victoria Lombardi

Age: 30

From: Miami

Address: 60 Beach Avenue

Cell No: 786-555-0174

You are Bae.

Name: Bae Park

Age: 24

From: Chicago

Address: 90 Clapton Road

Cell No: 312-555-0027

Unit 3 | Page 35, Exercise 6

Student B

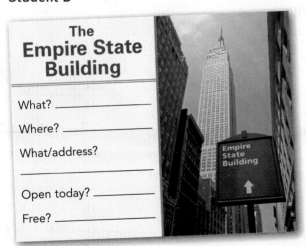

The Empire State Building

What? _____

Where? _____

What/address? _____

_____

Open today? _____

Free? _____

Universal Studios

Hollywood
100 Universal City Plaza
Los Angeles, CA

Admission $69

Open 7 days a week

L.A.'s big, exciting movie theme park!

Unit 4 | Page 47, Exercise 8b

Student B

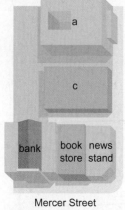
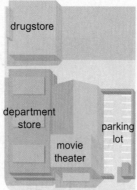

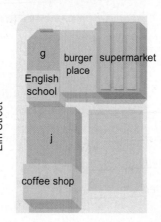

Mercer Street

Elm Street

a

c

drugstore

department store

parking lot

movie theater

bank

book store

news stand

restaurant

cell phone store

f

g

English school

burger place

supermarket

j

train station

coffee shop

Ask for:

- the sports store
- the shoe store
- the museum
- the bus station
- the City Hotel

Unit 6 | Page 63, Exercise 7

Student A

Name:	Sandra Young
From:	the US
Live in:	Vancouver, Canada
Reason here:	business
Job:	Sales rep (sell suitcases and backpacks to stores)
Work for:	The Big Bag Company
Work where:	near Vancouver
Husband:	William Young (Student B)

Student B

Name:	William Young
From:	Australia
Live in:	Vancouver, Canada
Reason here:	business
Job:	Sales rep (sell tea and coffee to supermarkets)
Work for:	Love Coffee Company
Work where:	in Vancouver
Wife:	Sandra Young (Student A)

Unit 7 | Page 71, Exercise 8b

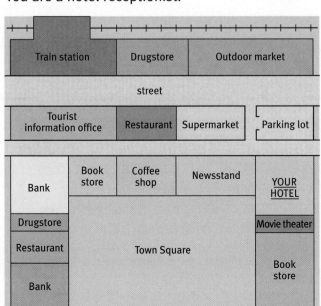

See page 112 for answers.

Unit 5 | Page 53, Exercise 5

Student A

You are a hotel receptionist.

| Train station | Drugstore | Outdoor market |

street

| Tourist information office | Restaurant | Supermarket | Parking lot |

Bank	Book store	Coffee shop	Newsstand	YOUR HOTEL
Drugstore				Movie theater
Restaurant	Town Square			Book store
Bank				

Unit 8 | Page 87, Exercise 6

Student A

Person	Address
Mr. M. Haddon	7 Oak Lane, 10a
Ms. A. Walker	7 Oak Lane, 9b
Ms. Z. Smith	7 Oak Lane, 8c
Mr. J. Heller	7 Oak Lane, 7b
Mr. S. Kato	7 Oak Lane, 7a

Unit 8 | Page 82, Exercise 3c

A good present for Pablo's sister: money

Unit 4 | Page 47, Exercise 8b

Student A

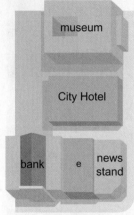
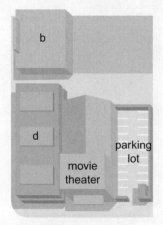
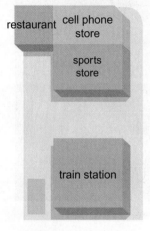
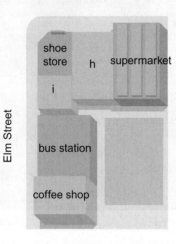

Ask for:

- the burger place
- the department store
- the drugstore
- the English school
- the bookstore

Unit 6 | Page 61, Exercise 6b

Student B

1. big cities
2. hip hop music
3. Nicole Kidman and Keith Urban
4. museums
5. Julia Roberts
6. Bill Gates
7. the countryside

Unit 7 | Page 71, Exercise 8b

Answers:

1. October/Fall
2. January/Winter
3. April/Spring
4. July/Summer

Unit 6 | Page 63, Exercise 7

Student C

Name:	Keiko Price
From:	Japan
Live in:	Tokyo, Japan
Reason here:	vacation
Job:	Bag designer
Work for:	Bags R Us
Work where:	in Tokyo
Husband:	Ron Price (Student D)

Student D

Name:	Ron Price
From:	the UK
Live in:	Tokyo, Japan
Reason here:	vacation
Job:	English teacher
Work for:	Gotham English school
Work where:	in Tokyo
Wife:	Keiko Price (Student C)

Unit 6 | Page 67, Exercise 8

findanicepresent.com

Unit 8 | Page 83, Exercise 6

Read the quiz questions. Check (✓) A, B, or C.

A = Yes, I do.

B = No, but I want one.

C = No, and I don't want one.

Technology Quiz	A	B	C
1. Do you have a computer?			
2. Do you have an MP3 player?			
3. Do you have a digital camera?			
4. Do you have a camera-phone?			
5. Do you have a phone with apps?			
6. Do you have a flat-screen TV?			
7. Do you have broadband on your TV?			
8. Do you have a GPS device?			
9. Do you have an e-book reader?			

Unit 8 | Page 85, Exercise 8

Students B and C

Salt and Pepper
Menu

APPETIZERS

Chicken salad

Vegetable soup

House salad

Seafood cocktail

MAIN COURSES

Beef with vegetables and rice

Lamb chops with rice

Roast chicken with potatoes

Seafood pasta

Fish with vegetables and rice

DESSERTS

Chocolate ice cream

Chocolate cake

Cheese and fruit

Unit 10 | Page 101, Exercise 9

The Story of the Mona Lisa
(PART 3)

Two years later, the police arrested Vincenzo Peruggia. He was the thief. But how did he steal the "Mona Lisa"? Vincenzo was in the Louvre on August 21, 1911. The museum was very quiet. When Vincenzo walked out, the "Mona Lisa" was under his coat. The painting stayed in Vincenzo's apartment, near the Louvre, for two years. In 1913, Vincenzo wanted to sell the painting. He wanted to sell it in Italy. The police arrested him in Milan.

Unit 5 | Page 53, Exercise 5

Student B

You are a hotel guest. Ask questions with *Is there a . . . near here?* or *Are there any . . . near here?* Complete the chart.

What?	Yes/No	Where?
Restaurant	*Yes (2)*	*1= across from the coffee shop* *2=next to the bank*
Outdoor market		
Bookstore		
Tourist information office		
Train station		
Bank		
Drugstore		

Unit 8 | Page 87, Exercise 6

Student B

Ms. M. Atwood	7 Oak Lane, 7c
Mr. J. Coe	7 Oak Lane, 8b
Ms. T. Morrison	7 Oak Lane, 8a
Mr. O. Pamuk	7 Oak Lane, 9c
Mrs. A. Garcia	7 Oak Lane, 9a

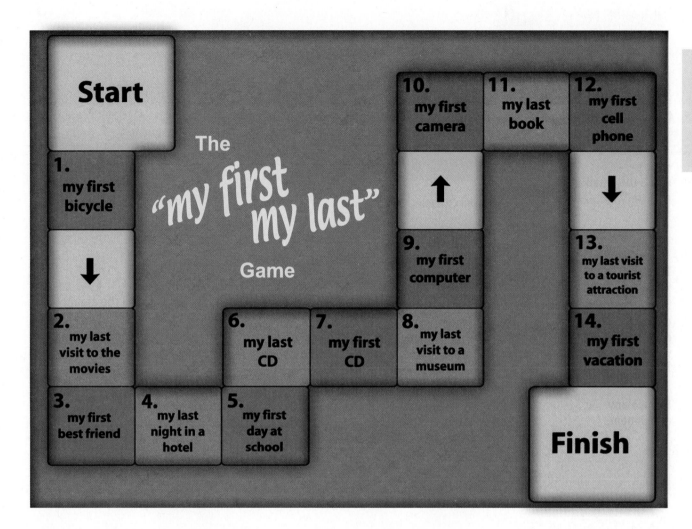

The "my first my last" Game

Start

1. my first bicycle

↓

2. my last visit to the movies

3. my first best friend

4. my last night in a hotel

5. my first day at school

6. my last CD

7. my first CD

8. my last visit to a museum

9. my first computer

10. my first camera

↑

11. my last book

12. my first cell phone

↓

13. my last visit to a tourist attraction

14. my first vacation

Finish

Writing Bank

A vacation email

Write a subject for your email.

Begin the email: *Hi* or *Hello* + name,

Talk about the place: your hotel/the town, etc. Use contractions: *we're, it's, . . .*

Explain any attachments.

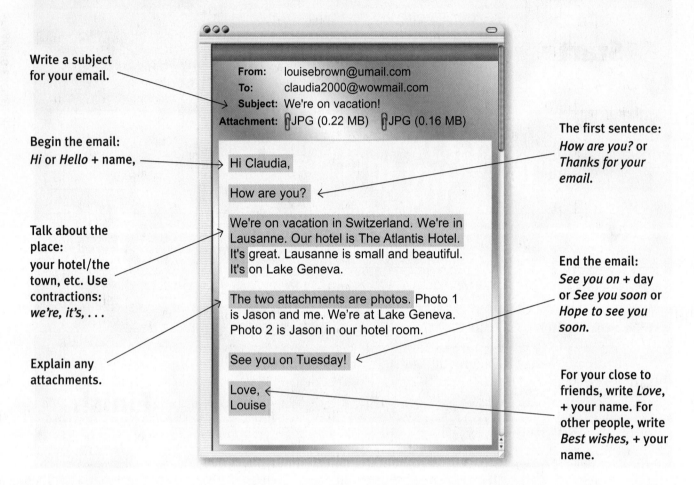

The first sentence: *How are you?* or *Thanks for your email.*

End the email: *See you on* + day or *See you soon* or *Hope to see you soon.*

For your close to friends, write *Love,* + your name. For other people, write *Best wishes,* + your name.

From: louisebrown@umail.com
To: claudia2000@wowmail.com
Subject: We're on vacation!
Attachment: JPG (0.22 MB) JPG (0.16 MB)

Hi Claudia,

How are you?

We're on vacation in Switzerland. We're in Lausanne. Our hotel is The Atlantis Hotel. It's great. Lausanne is small and beautiful. It's on Lake Geneva.

The two attachments are photos. Photo 1 is Jason and me. We're at Lake Geneva. Photo 2 is Jason in our hotel room.

See you on Tuesday!

Love,
Louise

Writing tip | punctuation

. = period   ? = a question mark
, = a comma   ' = an apostrophe
A, B, C, etc. = capital letters

Periods

Use a period at the end of a sentence.
- *Our hotel is The Atlantis Hotel.*

Capital letters

Use a capital letter at the beginning of a sentence.
- *The two attachments are photos.*

Use capital letters for the names of people, places, days, months, books, and movies.
- *My favorite author is Hemingway.*
- *See you on Thursday.*

Use a capital letter for the pronoun *I*.
- *Can I have a cup of coffee, please?*

Use capital letters for countries, nationalities, and languages.
- *She's from Spain. She's Spanish.*

Commas

Use commas in lists.
- *It's small, old, and beautiful.*
- *The attachment is a photo of Laura, Adam, and Sarah.*

Use a comma before *please* and after *yes* and *no*.
- *What's your name, please?*
- A: *Coffee?*   B: *No, thank you.*

Apostrophes

Use an apostrophe to show a contraction.
- *We are on vacation. → We're on vacation.*

Use an apostrophe + *s* to show possession.
- *Do you like Jason's car?*
- *They are Susan's books.*

A description | my favorite place to visit

Use capital letters for cities and countries: *New York, Mexico City, Japan*, etc.

My favorite place to visit is New York City. It's on the East Coast. There are a lot of museums, shops, restaurants, and other tourist attractions.

Use apostrophe + *s* (*'s*) to show possession: *New York's parks, Seoul's museums*, etc.

New York's parks are great. Central Park is in the center of New York. It's very big, and in summer there are concerts in the park. Bryant Park is beautiful, too. It's a small park near Grand Central Station.

Use adjectives to describe a place: *popular, great, modern, beautiful, old*, etc.

The Metropolitan Museum is very popular. It's very big, and the building is beautiful. But I think The Museum of Modern Art is New York's top attraction. It's in Midtown, near Fifth Avenue. The exhibitions are great!

Talk about location: *in, on, near, next to*, etc.

The Empire State Building is a popular tourist attraction. It's a very tall building. It's in Midtown, near Times Square. It's expensive, but the views of New York are amazing.

Writing tip | *and, but*

Use *and* before the last item in a list.

- *There are a lot of museums, shops, restaurants, <u>and</u> other tourist attractions.*
- *It's very big, very old, <u>and</u> very popular.*
- *He's an actor <u>and</u> a teacher.*

Use *and* to join two similar sentences.

- *The country is beautiful. The beaches are great.*
  - → *The country is beautiful, <u>and</u> the beaches are great.*
- *Central Park is very big. There are concerts in the park.*
  - → *Central Park is very big, <u>and</u> there are concerts in the park.*

Use *but* to join two different (contrasting) sentences.

- *The country is beautiful. The beaches are awful.*
  - → *The country is beautiful, <u>but</u> the beaches are awful.*
- *There's a museum in the town. There isn't a theme park.*
  - → *There's a museum in the town, <u>but</u> there isn't a theme park.*

A letter to a friend

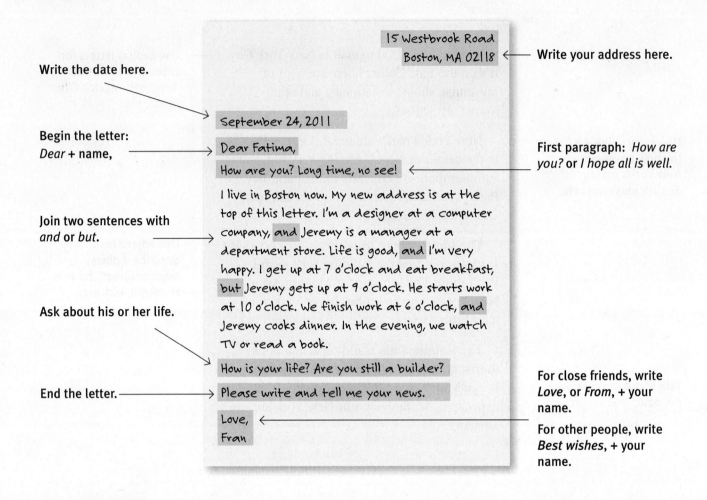

Write the date here.

Begin the letter: *Dear* + name,

Join two sentences with *and* or *but*.

Ask about his or her life.

End the letter.

15 Westbrook Road
Boston, MA 02118

Write your address here.

September 24, 2011

Dear Fatima,

How are you? Long time, no see!

I live in Boston now. My new address is at the top of this letter. I'm a designer at a computer company, and Jeremy is a manager at a department store. Life is good, and I'm very happy. I get up at 7 o'clock and eat breakfast, but Jeremy gets up at 9 o'clock. He starts work at 10 o'clock. We finish work at 6 o'clock, and Jeremy cooks dinner. In the evening, we watch TV or read a book.

How is your life? Are you still a builder?

Please write and tell me your news.

Love,
Fran

First paragraph: *How are you?* or *I hope all is well.*

For close friends, write *Love*, or *From*, + your name.

For other people, write *Best wishes*, + your name.

Writing tip | spelling of verbs in the simple present with *he/she/it*

With *he*, *she*, and *it*, add -*s* to the verb.
- *I get up early. He get<u>s</u> up late.*
- *I start work at nine o'clock. She start<u>s</u> work at ten o'clock.*

For verbs ending in -*ch*, -*sh*, -*s*, -*x*, -*z*, and -*o*, add -*es* to the verb with *he*, *she*, and *it*.
- *They watch TV. She watch<u>es</u> TV.*
- *I finish work at five o'clock. She finish<u>es</u> work at six o'clock.*

For verbs ending in consonant + -*y*, change *y* to *i* and add -*es*.
- *I carry the big bags, and my brother carr<u>ies</u> the small bags.*

For verbs ending in vowel + -*y*, add *s*.
- *I play tennis, and my sister play<u>s</u> basketball.*

A formal email

Write a subject for your email.

Don't use contractions.

End the email with *I look forward to your reply.*

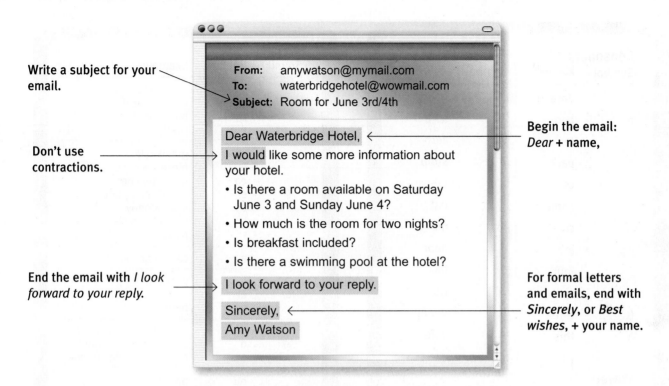

From: amywatson@mymail.com
To: waterbridgehotel@wowmail.com
Subject: Room for June 3rd/4th

Dear Waterbridge Hotel,

I would like some more information about your hotel.

• Is there a room available on Saturday June 3 and Sunday June 4?
• How much is the room for two nights?
• Is breakfast included?
• Is there a swimming pool at the hotel?

I look forward to your reply.

Sincerely,
Amy Watson

Begin the email: *Dear* + name,

For formal letters and emails, end with *Sincerely,* or *Best wishes,* + your name.

Writing tip | formal English and informal English

These are the main differences between formal English and informal English in writing.

INFORMAL Writing to a friend	FORMAL Writing to a business contact

Start with:
• *Hi* + first name,
  NOTE: we don't use
  • ~~Dear Friend,~~
  • ~~Hi Friend,~~
	Start with:
	• *Dear* + *Mr./Mrs./Miss/Ms.* + last name,
	When you don't know the person's name, start with:
	• *Dear Sir or Madam,*

Before you end the email use: • *See you soon.* • *Speak to you soon.*	Before you end the email, use: • *I look forward to your reply.* • *I look forward to hearing from you soon.*
End with: • *Love,* • *Take care,* When you don't know the person very well, end with: • *Best,* • *Best wishes,*	End with: • *Sincerely,* • *Best wishes,*
Use contractions: • *I'm, you're, they're,* etc.	Do not use contractions. Use: • *I am, you are, they are,* etc. **NOTE:** It is OK to use *don't.*

Pronunciation Bank

Part 1 | ▶ 2.45 English phonemes

Part 2 | ▶ 2.46 Sound-spelling correspondences

Consonants

Symbol	Key word	Symbol	Key word
d	**d**ate	ŋ	goi**ng**
b	**b**ed	s	**s**ofa
t	**t**en	z	**z**ero
p	**p**ark	ʃ	**sh**op
k	**c**ar	ʒ	televi**si**on
g	**g**ame	h	**h**at
tʃ	**ch**ild	m	**m**enu
dʒ	**j**ob	n	**n**ear
f	**f**our	l	**l**ike
v	**v**isit	r	**r**ide
θ	**th**ree	y	**y**oung
ð	**th**is	w	**w**ife

Vowels

Symbol	Key word	Symbol	Key word
i	b**e**	ə	**a**bout
ɪ	s**i**t	eɪ	d**ay**
ɛ	r**e**d	aɪ	b**y**
æ	c**a**t	aʊ	h**ou**se
ɑ	f**a**ther	ɔɪ	b**oy**
oʊ	b**oa**t	ɑr	c**ar**
ɔ	b**ou**ght	ɔr	d**oor**
ʊ	b**oo**k	ʊr	t**our**
u	sh**oe**	ɪr	h**ere**
ʌ	b**u**t	ɛr	th**ere**
ɚ	w**or**d		

Sound	Spelling	Examples
/ɪ/	i	th**i**s l**i**sten
	y	g**y**m t**y**pical
	ui	b**ui**ld g**ui**tar
	e	pr**e**tty
/i/	ee	gr**ee**n sl**ee**p
	ie	n**ie**ce bel**ie**ve
	ea	r**ea**d t**ea**cher
	e	th**e**se compl**e**te
	ey	k**ey** mon**ey**
	ei	rec**ei**pt rec**ei**ve
	i	pol**i**ce
/æ/	a	c**a**n m**a**n l**a**nd
/ɑ/	a	p**a**sta
	al	c**al**m
	ea	h**ea**rt
/ʌ/	u	f**u**n s**u**nny h**u**sband
	o	s**o**me m**o**ther m**o**nth
	ou	c**ou**sin d**ou**ble y**ou**ng
/ɔ/	ou	b**ou**ght
	au	d**au**ghter t**au**ght
	al	b**al**d sm**al**l **al**ways
	aw	dr**aw** jigs**aw**
/aɪ/	i	l**i**ke t**i**me **i**sland
	y	dr**y** sh**y** c**y**cle
	ie	fr**ie**s d**ie** t**ie**
	igh	l**igh**t h**igh** r**igh**t
	ei	h**ei**ght
	ey	**ey**es
	uy	b**uy**
/ɛɪ/	a	l**a**ke h**a**te sh**a**ve
	ai	w**ai**t tr**ai**n str**ai**ght
	ay	pl**ay** s**ay** st**ay**
	ey	th**ey** ob**ey**
	ei	**ei**ght w**ei**ght
	ea	br**ea**k
/oʊ/	o	h**o**me ph**o**ne **o**pen
	ow	sh**ow** thr**ow** **ow**n
	oa	c**oa**t r**oa**d c**oa**st
	ol	c**o**ld t**o**ld

Part 3 | ▶ 2.47 Syllable stress

Words with more than one syllable have the stress on one of the syllables.

1–syllable words ●	**2–syllable words** ●○	**2–syllable words** ○●
one six big young read learn friend great lake house beach road west	happy seven listen morning passport father website photo awful teacher picture modern Sunday	Japan address between today behind Chinese design July explain mistake dessert because
3–syllable words ●○○	**3–syllable words** ○●○	**3–syllable words** ○○●
Italy favorite beautiful Saturday visitor medium popular interview architect hospital	eleven computer cathedral espresso attachment important piano designer reporter together September tomorrow exciting potato	afternoon engineer introduce

Part 4 | ▶ 2.48 Questions

We often use weak forms at the beginning of questions.

<u>Are you</u> at home?	/ər yə/
<u>Are they</u> ready?	/ər ðeɪ/
<u>Do you</u> like it?	/də yə/
<u>Do you</u> write reports?	/də yə/
<u>What do you</u> do?	wədiyə
<u>Where do they</u> work?	wɛrdiyə
<u>Are you going to</u> get married?	/ər yə ɡoʊɪŋ tə/
	or /ər yə ɡənə/
<u>Are you going to</u> call her?	/ər yə ɡoʊɪŋ tə/
	or /ər yə ɡənə/
<u>Were you</u> a good student?	/wɚ yə/
<u>Did you</u> see him?	/dɪ dʒə/
<u>Did you</u> talk to her?	/dɪ dʒə/

Irregular Verbs

Verb	Simple Past	Past Participle
be	was/were	been
become	became	become
begin	began	begun
break	broke	broken
bring	brought	brought
build	built	built
buy	bought	bought
can	could	been able
catch	caught	caught
choose	chose	chosen
come	came	come
cost	cost	cost
dig	dug	dug
do	did	done
draw	drew	drawn
drink	drank	drunk
drive	drove	driven
eat	ate	eaten
fall	fell	fallen
feed	fed	fed
feel	felt	felt
find	found	found
fly	flew	flown
forget	forgot	forgotten
get	got	got
give	gave	given
go	went	gone/been
grow	grew	grown
have	had	had
hear	heard	heard
hold	held	held
hurt	hurt	hurt
keep	kept	kept
know	knew	known
learn	learned/learnt	learned/learnt

Verb	Simple Past	Past Participle
leave	left	left
let	let	let
lose	lost	lost
make	made	made
mean	meant	meant
meet	met	met
pay	paid	paid
put	put	put
read/rid/	read/red/	read/red/
ride	rode	ridden
ring	rang	rung
run	ran	run
say	said	said
see	saw	seen
sell	sold	sold
send	sent	sent
shine	shone	shone
show	showed	shown
sing	sang	sung
sit	sat	sat
sleep	slept	slept
speak	spoke	spoken
spend	spent	spent
stand	stood	stood
steal	stole	stolen
swim	swam	swum
take	took	taken
teach	taught	taught
tell	told	told
think	thought	thought
throw	threw	thrown
understand	understood	understood
wear	wore	worn
win	won	won
write	wrote	written

Audioscript

▶ 1.02 (Page 6)
1. supermarket 2. restaurant
3. movie theater 4. camera 5. doctor
6. soccer 7. bus 8. television
9. pizza 10. tennis 11. taxi 12. police
13. university 14. telephone 15. hotel

▶ 1.05 (Page 8)
1. listen 2. read 3. write 4. speak
5. match 6. repeat 7. look

UNIT 1 Introductions

▶ 1.09 (Page 11)
D=David B=Betty C=Carla J=Jeff
F=Friends
1.
D: Good morning.
B: Good morning.
2.
D: Good afternoon.
C: Good afternoon.
3.
D: Good evening.
J: Good evening.
4.
D: Good night.
F: Good night.

▶ 1.11 (Page 12)
1. China 2. Australia 3. Argentina
4. Japan 5. the US 6. Brazil
7. the UK 8. Spain 9. Italy
10. Colombia

▶ 1.12 (Page 13)
1. She's Shakira. She's from Colombia.
   She's in Portugal.
2. He's Johnny Depp. He's from the US.
   He's in Japan.
3. She's Penelope Cruz. She's from Spain.
   She's in the US.

▶ 1.13 (Page 14)
L=Luisa B=Boris A=Andy
A: Hi Boris.
B: Hi, Andy. This is Luisa.
A: Nice to meet you, Luisa.
L: Nice to meet you, too.

▶ 1.14 (Page 14)
A=Andy L=Luisa
L: Where are you from, Andy?
A: I'm from the US.
L: Where are you from in the US?
A: I'm from New York. Where are you from?
L: I'm from Argentina.
A: Where are you from in Argentina?
L: I'm from Rosario.

▶ 1.16 (Page 15)
1.
A: Coffee?
B: Yes, please.
2.
A: Black pepper?
B: No, thank you.

3.
A: I'm hungry.
B: Excuse me . . .
4.
A: He's Ronaldinho from Brazil.
B: Pardon?

▶ 1.17 (Page 17)
Australia: six, one.
Brazil: five, five.
China: eight, six.
Japan: eight, one.
Mexico: five, two.
Russia: seven.
Spain: three, four.
Turkey: nine, zero.
the UK: four, four.
the US: one.

▶ 1.18 (Page 17)
W=Woman M=Man Mch=Machine
W: Directory assistance.
M: The Royal Hawaiian, please.
W: Where is it?
M: It's in Honolulu, Hawaii.
W: Thank you.
Mch: The number is: five-five-five, eight-
      nine-two, three-zero-one-one.

UNIT 2 Family and friends

▶ 1.19 (Page 19)
1. phone number   3. laptop
2. email address 4. passport
9. address   7. first name
6. cell phone   8. last name   5. map

▶ 1.20 (Page 20)
L=Liz S=Sabrina
L: Ooh! Who's he?
S: Carl? He's my brother. He's 26 years old.
L: Twenty-six? He's cute.
S: Thanks. And she's my sister, Anna. She's
   twenty-two. And he's my father, Marek.
   He's sixty.
L: Who's she?
S: She's my mother, Sofia. She's from Italy.
   She's fifty-seven. And my daughter,
   Sarah. She's almost one. And my son,
   Tom. He's three.
L: Oh! Who's he?
S: He's my husband, James.
L: Oh! How old is he?
S: He's thirty-eight.

▶ 1.24 (Page 22)
B=Ben J1=Judge 1 J2=Judge 2
B: Hello.
J1/J2: Hello.
J1:   What's your name?
B: Ben Gibson.
J1:   How do you spell that?
B: Gibson. G – I – B – S – O – N
J1:   Where are you from, Ben?
B: I'm from Los Angeles.
J1:   How old are you?

B: I'm twenty-nine.
J2:   What's your address?
B: Seventeen Melrose Street.
J1:   What's your phone number?
B: My home number is three-two-three,
       five-five-five, zero-one-five-four. And
       my cell number is three-one-oh, five-
       five-five, zero-zero-nine-eight.
J1/J2: Thank you.
J2:   OK, Mr. Gibson!
B: Oh! OK! Yes . . .
B: Every morning, she's on my train,
       where is she from, and what's her
       name.

▶ 1.25 (Page 23)
1.
A: What's your name, please?
B: Simon Ambrose.
A: How do you spell that?
B: Ambrose. A – M – B – R – O – S – E.
2.
A: What's your address, please?
B: 82 via Speranza, Rome.
A: How do you spell that, please?
B: Via: V – I – A. Speranza: S – P – E – R –
   A – N – Z – A.

▶ 1.26 (Page 23)
J1=Judge 1 J2=Judge 2 J3=Judge 3
J4=Judge 4 J5=Judge 5
Be=Ben T=Terri V=Victoria Ba=Bae
1.
Be: Every morning, she's on my train, where
    is she from, and what's her name.
J1: Thank you. Ben. Goodbye. He's awful.
J2: Yes, awful.
J3/J4: Yeah. Uh-huh.
2.
T: I am in love with you, in love with you.
J3: Thank you, Terri.
T: OK. Thank you. Goodbye.
J3: Goodbye. She's good.
J2: Yes, she's good.
J3/J4: Yeah. Uh-hmm.
3.
V: I am in love with you, in love with you.
J1: Thank you Victoria.
V: Oh, thank you.
J1: Goodbye.
V: Goodbye.
J1: She's OK.
J4: Yes, she's OK.
J3/J5: Yeah.
4.
Ba: I am in love with you, in love with you.
J3: Thank you Bae. Thank you.
Ba: OK. Thank you. Goodbye.
J3: He's great!
J2: Yes, he's great.
J3/J4: Mm-hmm. Yeah.

A: What's the website?
B: w-w-w dot emailfriends dot net
A: Uh-huh. Who's she?
B: Her name's Frieda Lang.
A: What's her occupation?
B: She's a teacher.
A: What's her email address?
B: frieda@teachernet.de
A: What's his name?
B: Tom Mackintosh.
A: What's his occupation?
B: Uh . . . He's an accountant.
A: What's his email address?
B: It's tom@mackintosh.com.
A: Hmm . . . What's her name?
B: Her name's Junko Nakamura. She's a student.
A: Oh! I'm a student, too. What's her email address?
B: junura@jmail.jp
A: How do you spell that?
B: Junura: J – U – N – U – R – A, at jmail: J – M – A – I – L dot J – P.
A: Thank you!

▶ **1.28** (Page 25)

8. accountant 4. student 5. actor
10. manager 7. engineer 9. sales clerk
3. teacher 6. police officer 2. artist
1. doctor

UNIT 3 Traveling

▶ **1.30** (Page 32)

2. a camera 9. a T-shirt 1. a book
6. a map 7. a skirt 4. a blouse
5. a sweater 8. an MP3 player
10. a suitcase 3. a backpack
12. a pair of pants 11. a pair of shoes

▶ **1.31** (Page 32)

C=Customs R=Ron D=Diane E=Eva
1.
C: What's in your suitcase, sir?
R: What's in my suitcase? Um, a map, a camera, two books, a shirt, and two pairs of pants. Oh, and a pair of shoes.
2.
C: What's in your suitcase, ma'am?
D: Oh, uh, let me see. A camera – no! Two cameras, an MP3 player, a pair of shoes, two skirts, two blouses, a sweater, three books, and a backpack.
3.
C: What's in your suitcase, miss?
E: What's in my suitcase? Umm, a camera, two maps, two books, two blouses, a sweater, an MP3 player, a pair of pants and a skirt and . . . um . . . five pairs of shoes.

▶ **1.32** (Page 32)

C=Customs E=Eva
C: What's in your suitcase, Miss?
E: What's in my suitcase? Umm, a camera, two maps, two books, two blouses, a sweater, an MP3 player, a pair of pants and a skirt and . . . um . . . five pairs of shoes.

▶ **1.34** (Page 33)

C=Customs J=Jane Smith
C: Excuse me. What's your name?
J: Jane Smith.
C: What's in your suitcase, Miss Smith?
J: I'm not Miss Smith. I'm Ms. Smith.
C: Sorry. OK, a camera . . .
J: It isn't a camera. It's an MP3 player.
C: An MP3 player . . . and two books . . .
J: They aren't books. They're maps.

▶ **1.36** (Page 34)

H=Hotel Clerk W=Woman
H: Good morning.
W: Good morning. Is the museum open today?
H: Yes, it is.
W: Is it near here?
H: Yes, it is. It's just off Fifth Avenue.
W: Oh, OK.
H: It's about six blocks from here. Here's a map. We're here, and it's there.
W: Is the museum free?
H: No, it isn't. Admission is twenty dollars.

UNIT 4 Stores and restaurants

▶ **1.38** (Page 39)

C. ATM H. bank K. bus stop
I. drugstore G. bookstore
A. restaurant J. supermarket
D. newsstand F. parking lot
B. train station E. movie theater
L. outdoor market

▶ **1.39** (Page 40)

1.
A: Hello. Can I help you?
B: Yes. Can I have a house salad, please?
A: Certainly. Anything else?
B: Yes. Can I have a large bottled water, too?
A: Sure.
2.
A: Good afternoon.
B: Good afternoon. A cheese sandwich and a small orange juice.
A: Anything else?
B: No, thank you.
A: To eat here?
B: Pardon?
A: To eat here or take out?
B: Oh, take out, please.
3.
A: Yes, sir. Can I help you?
B: Yes, can I have a cup of tea and a piece of chocolate cake, please?
A: Certainly. Anything else?
B: No, that's it.
A: So, one cup of tea and one piece of chocolate cake.
B: Thank you.
A: No problem.

▶ **1.41** (Page 41)

1. a dollar ten
2. three dollars and ninety-eight cents
3. eight dollars and nineteen cents
4. fifty-euros seventy
5. four euros and forty-three
6. three pounds thirty-nine pence

▶ **1.42** (Page 42)

1. a green T-shirt 2. a pair of white shoes
3. an orange dress 4. a red coat
5. a yellow hat 6. a pair of black pants
7. a blue bag 8. a brown skirt
9. a pink blouse

▶ **1.43** (Page 43)

S=Sales clerk C=Claudia
S: Hello. Can I help you?
C: Yes, how much is this blue hat?
S: It's $25.
C: Ooh! And how much are these beautiful dresses?
S: They're $99.95.
C: How much is that yellow skirt?
S: It's $68.99.
C: Sixty-eight ninety-nine? How much are those white shirts?
S: They're $35. The orange shirts are $40.

▶ **1.44** (Page 44)

1.
A: Can I have three tickets to Boston, please? Two adults and one child.
B: One-way or round-trip?
A: Round-trip, please.
B: That's $42.30, please. Thank you. Here you are.
2.
A: Can I have two tickets for *Legally Blonde*, please?
B: That's $98.90, please.
A: Can I pay by credit card?
B: Sure. Sign here, please. Thank you. Here you are.
A: Thanks.
3.
A: Your groceries come to $31.07.
B: Here you are. It's a debit card.
A: Enter your PIN number, please. Thank you.

▶ **1.45** (Page 47)

1.
A: Excuse me. Where is the cell phone store?
B: Um . . . Let me see. It's next to the restaurant on Mercer Street.
A: Great. Thank you.
B: You're welcome.
2.
A: Excuse me. Where's the train station?
B: I'm sorry, I don't know.
A: OK. Thanks anyway. Excuse me, where's the train station?
C: The train station? . . . It's on Elm Street, across from the coffee shop.
A: Great. Thank you.
C: You're welcome.
3.
A: Excuse me. Where's the nearest supermarket?
B: Uh, the nearest supermarket is across from the parking lot on Mercer Street.
A: Great. Thank you.
B: No problem.

UNIT 5 Things to see and do

▶ 1.46 (Page 49)

1. Darwin is in the north of Australia.
2. Perth is in the west of Australia.
3. Brisbane is in the east of Australia.
4. Adelaide is in the south of Australia.
5. Alice Springs is in the center of Australia.

▶ 1.48 (Page 52)

1. The bookstore is next to the Italian restaurant.
2. The coffee shop is in front of the train station.
3. The drugstore is across from the shoe store.
4. The theater is near the hotel.
5. The parking lot is behind the department store.

▶ 1.49 (Page 52)

R=Receptionist M=Man W=Woman

R: Hello sir, ma'am. Can I help you?
M: Yes. Is there a coffee shop near this hotel?
R: Yes, sir, there is. There's a coffee shop behind this hotel and there's another coffee shop in front of the train station.
W: Are there any good restaurants near here?
R: Yes, there are. There's a good Mexican restaurant next to the hotel. There's a Chinese restaurant across from the museum that's very good. And there's an Italian restaurant next to the bookstore. There's also a good seafood restaurant called the Blue Fin Grill across from the Italian restaurant.
M: Great. And, is there a bank near here?
R: Yes, sir, there is. There's a bank next to the theater, but it isn't open today.
M: Oh no!
R: But there's an ATM in this hotel. It's right over there.
M: Great!
W: Are there any tourist attractions near here?
R: Yes, ma'am, there are. There's the museum near the train station, across from the Chinese restaurant. Here's a map. We're here, and the museum is here.
W: Great. Thank you.
R: You're welcome.

▶ 1.50 (Page 53)

Chez Pierre is a French restaurant.
The Taj Mahal is an Indian restaurant.
La Spiga is an Italian restaurant.
Wong Li is a Chinese restaurant.
Azteca is a Mexican restaurant.
Sushi Taro is a Japanese restaurant.

▶ 1.51 (Page 54)

P=Peter C=Carla

P: Hi, Carla. How are you?
C: Fine, thanks. And you?
P: I'm OK. Are you here for the summer classes?
C: Yes, I am.
P: OK, these are our summer classes. They're "English Plus" classes. They're English plus another class.
C: OK.

P: Here's one. Can you drive?
C: Yes, I can drive.
P: All right. Can you swim?
C: Yes, I can. But I can't play golf . . . golf isn't my favorite sport.
P: OK. Well, can you cook?
C: Yes, I can cook. And I can use a computer, and I can dance.
P: Hmm . . . Can you sing?
C: Yes, I can sing. But I can't play the piano.
P: Is that interesting to you?
C: Yes.
P: Is two to four in the afternoon OK for you?
C: Yes, that's fine.
P: OK, Carla. It's open. Class 173 it is.

▶ 1.52 (Page 55)

1. I can cook.   2. I can't swim.
3. I can play the piano.   4. I can't sing.
5. I can drive.

▶ 1.54 (Page 57)

T=Teresa N=Nick B=Brenda

T: Welcome to our B and B. I'm Teresa. Nice to meet you.
N/B: Nice to meet you, too.
T: Come with me. Your bedroom is this way. So, where are you from?
N: We're from Texas.
T: Well, welcome to the mountains. This is your bedroom. There's a king-sized bed, and the bathroom is here.
B: Oh, this looks nice.
T: And there's a hot tub outside. Come with me. It's right out here.
B: This is a very nice house.
T: Thanks very much. Here we are: the hot tub.
N: Oh, wow. That's great.
B: There's a nice view of the mountains.
T: The hot tub is open from eight thirty in the morning to ten thirty at night.
B: OK.
T: And there's a free continental breakfast in the morning–croissants, fruit, coffee, and orange juice.
B: Great. What time is that?
T: Breakfast is from seven fifteen to ten fifteen in the dining room.
N: OK, sounds good. And what time is checkout?
T: Checkout is at eleven forty-five.
B: OK, thanks.

UNIT 6 All about you

▶ 2.03 (Page 60)

DJ= Disk Jockey JDS= João da Silva

DJ: Now it's time for our 60-second interview.
Today João da Silva is in the studio. Welcome to *Radio Chicago*, João.
JDS: Thank you.
DJ: João . . . your 60-second interview starts . . . now.
DJ: So, João What do you do? What's your occupation?
JDS: I'm a singer.
DJ: Where are you from?
JDS: I'm from Bahia, but Rio de Janeiro is my home now.
DJ: Do you like Chicago?

JDS: Yes, I do. It's very nice.
DJ: You're a singer. Do you like American hip hop music?
JDS: No, not really. I like Brazilian music, especially samba.
DJ: OK. What's your favorite sport?
JDS: Soccer, of course! I'm Brazilian.
DJ: Of course. What about food? Do you like Indian food?
JDS: No, I don't. I like French food.
DJ: What are your favorite things in life?
JDS: I like Brazilian music, German cars, Italian fashion . . .
DJ: Ah! Time is up. Thank you João da Silva!
JDS: You're welcome.
DJ: That was our 60-second interview!

▶ 2.04 (Page 60)

1. Do you like Italian food?
2. Do you like coffee?
3. Are you from Brazil?
4. Are you a student?

▶ 2.06 (Page 62)

1. Architects design buildings.
2. Sales reps sell things.
3. Fashion designers design clothes.
4. Reporters write articles.
5. Chefs cook food.
6. Construction workers build buildings.

▶ 2.07 (Page 62)

S=Sharon C=Catherine
P=Pat A=Anthony

S: Excuse me. Your coat is on the floor.
C: Pardon?
S: Your coat. It's on the floor.
C: Oh, yeah. Thanks a lot.
S: No problem! Are you here on vacation?
C: Yes, I am. I'm here with my husband. He's in our room. We really like this city.
S: Yes, it's great. By the way, my name's Sharon.
C: Hi, Sharon. I'm Catherine.
S: So where are you from?
C: I'm from Canada and my husband is from Australia. We live in Toronto. Where are you from?
S: We're from the US. We live in Seattle.
C: Are you here on vacation?
S: No, we aren't. We're here on business.
C: What do you do?
S: We're architects.
C: That's nice. What kinds of things do you design?
S: We design houses and office buildings.
C: I'm a sales rep and my husband is a chef.
S: Oh, really? What do you sell?
C: I sell clothing to department stores.
P: And who do you work for?
C: It's a small Canadian company. It's called PDS Fashions.
S: Oh, I'm sorry. This is my husband, Pat.
C: Nice to meet you. My name's Catherine. Ah! Here's my husband. Anthony, this is Sharon and Pat. They're from the US.
A: Nice to meet you.
P: Nice to meet you, too.
C: Sharon and Pat are architects. They design houses and office buildings.
A: Oh really? Where do you work?

▶ **2.08** (Page 67)

J=Jim N=Nancy

J: Oh, man!
N: What's the problem, Jim?
J: I can't find a present for Luz.
N: Who's Luz?
J: She's my friend. It's her birthday on Thursday.
N: Do you know www.findanicepresent.com?
J: No. What is it?
N: It's a great website. It finds presents for you. Look. This is the website.

▶ **2.09** (Page 67)

J=Jim N=Nancy

J: Is it free?
N: Yes, it is. OK, there are some questions here. Tell me about Luz. How old is she?
J: She's, um, twenty-nine.
N: And what does she do?
J: She's a reporter.
N: Who does she work for?
J: *Newstime* magazine.
N: She's a reporter. OK. So does she work long hours?
J: Yes, she does.
N: Is she married?
J: No, she isn't.
N: What about children? Does she have any children?
J: No, she doesn't.
N: How about travel? Does she travel a lot?
J: Yes. She travels all over the world.
N: She's lucky. Can she cook?
J: No, she can't.
N: How about movies? Does she watch a lot of movies?
J: Let me think. No, she doesn't.
N: Does she listen to a lot of music?
J: Yes. She loves music.
N: OK—there are three good presents on this website.

UNIT 7 A day at work

▶ **2.10** (Page 69)

1. F. I'm a waiter. I work in a restaurant.
2. A. I'm an office worker. I work in an office.
3. G. I'm a factory worker. I work in a factory.
4. B. I'm a nurse. I work in a hospital.
5. E. I'm a sales clerk. I work in a shop.
6. C. I'm a professor. I work in a university.
7. D. I'm a researcher. I work in a lab.
8. H. I'm a teacher. I work in a school.

▶ **2.11** (Page 70)

1.

R=Receptionist J=Jake A=Alice S=Steven

R: Hello. Parkside School.
J: Can I speak to Mrs. Fisher, please?
R: Hold on, please.
A: Hello. Alice Fisher.
J: Hello, Mrs. Fisher. My name's Jake Parker. I'm interested in the teaching job. It's in today's newspaper . . .
A: Oh, yes. Great.

2.

A: Jake Parker?
J: Yes.
A: I'm Alice Fisher. Nice to meet you.
J: Nice to meet you, too.
A: Come in, Mr. Parker. Please sit down.
J: Thank you.

3.

J: OK, class, be quiet. Look at page 32 in your books. Page 32. OK? Now listen to the conversation.
J: Steven. Please turn off your cell phone.
S: Sorry.

▶ **2.12** (Page 71)

M=Man W=Woman

1.

M: Please come with me. Your table is ready.

2.

W: Taylor! Be QUIET.

3.

W: This is a message for Dr. Morgan. Please go to Room 200 immediately.

4.

M: This is a customer announcement. Visit our great kitchen sale on the ground floor. Saucepans for nineteen ninety-nine, cookbooks for six ninety-nine. Thank you for shopping at Madisons.

5.

W: This is a message for all passengers on flight FH453 to Hong Kong. Please go to gate 23 immediately. That's flight FH453. Please go to gate 23 immediately. Thank you.

▶ **2.14** (Page 72)

H=Game show host J=John

H: I'm Susan Sullivan and welcome to *What's your job?* Today we have John with us. Hi, John. Are you ready?
J: Yes, I'm always ready!
H: OK, let's start. Do you attend meetings?
J: Yes, I sometimes attend meetings.
H: Do you give presentations?
J: Yes, I often give presentations.
H: Do you call customers?
J: Yes, I usually call customers.
H: Do you write reports?
J: Yes, I do, but I don't often write reports.
H: Do you travel for work?
J: Yes, I sometimes travel for work.
H: Do you answer the phone?
J: Yes, I always answer the phone.
H: Do you work outside?
J: No, I never work outside.
H: Do you help people?
J: Yes, I often help people.
H: Are you a . . . sales rep?
J: Yes, I am!

▶ **2.16** (Page 74)

M=Michelle S=Sarah

M: Good morning, Sarah!
S: Morning, Michelle. Nice weekend?
M: Yes, thank you. And you?
S: Good, thanks.
M: Oh, Sarah, when is Mr. Wu's visit?
S: Let me see. Mr. Wu's visit is June 8th.
M: What's the date today?
S: It's June 6th.

M: Are there any other visits this month?
S: Um, yes, there are. There's Mrs. King on June 14th.
M: Mrs. King – June 14th.
S: And there's Ms. Brown on June 24th.
M: OK, June 24th. Is that all?
S: No, there's one more. It's Mr. Rodriguez.
M: Mr. Rodriguez – he's the big boss from Bogotá! He's very important! When is his visit?
S: June 6th.
M: June 6th?! . . . But, but that's today.
S: Uh-huh. Hello, Sarah Walker speaking. Hello Mr. Rodriguez. You're at the reception desk? Great. See you in five minutes. Goodbye. That's Mr. Rodriguez. He's at the reception desk.
M: Ugh!

▶ **2.18** (Page 75)

M=Michelle R=Mr. Rodriguez K=Ms. Khan

M: Please, come in. Have a seat. What would you like to drink? Tea? Coffee?
R: I'd like coffee.
K: I'd like a cup of tea, please.
M: Would you like milk or sugar?
R: No, thank you.
K: Milk, no sugar, please.

▶ **2.19** (Page 75)

M=Michelle R=Mr. Rodriguez K=Ms. Khan

M: All right. Well, this is the company cafeteria. Are you hungry?
R/K: Yes.
M: Good. OK, the drinks are here on the right. And there are snacks next to the drinks. There's bottled water, orange juice, etc. There are some appetizers next to the snacks. Would you like an appetizer?
R: Um, no thank you. I think I'd like a salad.
M: OK. There's a salad bar in the middle of the cafeteria.
K: I'd like some fruit.
M: The fruit is over there, next to the salad. And there are some desserts next to the cash register.
R: Great. Thank you.

▶ **2.20** (Page 77)

R=Receptionist WJL= Woo-jin Lee

R: Good morning. Can I help you?
WJL: Good morning. I'm here to see Martina Hafner.
R: Do you have an appointment?
WJL: Yes.
R: What's your name, please?
WJL: Woo-jin Lee.
R: How do you spell that?
WJL: W-O-O J-I-N Lee. L-E-E.
R: OK, Mr. Lee. Take the elevator to the third floor. Turn right. Ms. Hafner's office is the third door on the left.
WJL: Thank you.
R: You're welcome.

R=Receptionist J=James

R: Good morning.
J: Good morning. I have a meeting with Lorda Romero.
R: What's your name, please?
J: James Wood.

R: James – Wood. OK, Mr. Wood. Take the elevator to the third floor. Turn right. Mrs. Romero's office is the second on the right.
J: Thank you.

R=Receptionist J=Jessica
R: Good afternoon.
J: Good afternoon. I'm here to see Patrick Swinton.
R: Do you have an appointment?
J: Yes, I do.
R: What's your name, please?
J: My name's Jessica Hayes.
R: How do you spell Hayes?
J: H – A – Y – E – S.
R: OK, Ms. Hayes. Mr. Swinton's office is on the third floor. Take the elevator and turn right. It's the first door on the left.
J: Thank you.

UNIT 8 Your likes and dislikes

▶ **2.21** (Page 79)
1. go to the theater   2. go out to eat
3. play chess   4. go swimming
5. play soccer   6. go hiking
7. watch TV   8. go sightseeing
9. read a book   10. play tennis
11. go cycling   12. work out

▶ **2.22** (Page 80)
G=Gary A=Annie
A: Gary.
G: Yeah?
A: Are you happy?
G: Happy?
A: Yes. Are you happy?
G: Yeah. I'm happy.
A: I'm not. I'm bored. We never go out.
G: Oh.
A: We never go to the theater. We don't go sightseeing or stay at hotels. We never go out to eat. We always just stay home and watch television.
G: But I like watching television.
A: Gary!

▶ **2.23** (Page 80)
G=Gary A=Annie
G: OK . . . So, let's go away next weekend.
A: Go away?
G: Yes. What about going to Yosemite? We can go hiking, we can see the views. We can go biking, or go swimming.
A: Hmm . . . I don't want to go hiking. I want to go out to eat, I want to go shopping, I want to go to the theater. What about San Francisco?
G: San Francisco?
A: Yes, we can go sightseeing and see the city. You like to go sightseeing.
G: Yes, but, I don't like to go sightseeing in cities. I like going hiking, swimming, playing tennis—outdoor things.
A: Hmm . . . Well what about Palm Springs? You can go swimming—you like to swim. And we can play tennis, maybe some golf. And I can go shopping. And we can go out to eat.
G: You like to go out to eat . . . OK, I want to go to Palm Springs.

▶ **2.24** (Page 80)
I want to go out to eat.
I want to go shopping.
I want to go to the theater.
I don't want to go hiking.

▶ **2.25** (Page 82)
J. dishwasher   N. coffee table
G. mirror   L. sofa   M. lamp
E. toilet   B. bed   P. car   F. sink
Q. bicycle   I. cabinet   K. fridge
D. bathtub   A. window   H. stove
C. wardrobe   O. armchair

▶ **2.26** (Page 82)
P=Pablo J=Jo
P: Hi, Jo. How are you?
J: Oh, hi Pablo. I'm fine. How are you?
P: Oh, so-so. It's my sister's wedding next week and I want to buy her a really nice present, but I can't find one.
J: I can help.
P: Really?
J: Sure.
P: Thanks a lot.
J: No problem. What does she like doing?
P: Well, she likes doing things at home: she likes watching TV, she likes cooking. Oh, and she likes modern furniture. Her husband likes furniture, too.
J: Do they have an armchair?
P: Yes, they do.
J: Do they have a lamp?
P: Yes, they do.
J: Does your sister have a nice sofa?
P: No, she doesn't.
J: Buy her a sofa.
P: But my parents want to buy a nice sofa for her.
J: Oh, too bad. Well, do they have a coffee table?
P: Yes.
J: Okay, then does she have a bicycle?
P: No, she doesn't.
J: There you are.
P: But he has a bicycle and he uses it.
J: Oh . . . I know!
P: What?
J: It's always a good wedding present.
P: What?
J: Give them . . .

▶ **2.27** (Page 84)
M=Mark A=Anna
M: Hi, Anna.
A: Hi, Mark. What's new?
M: I got a new job!
A: Hey, that's great! Congratulations. How about dinner next Friday? We can celebrate.
M: Good idea. Which restaurant do you want to go to?
A: How about Sinatra's?
M: Where's that?
A: It's in Melrose.
M: Hmm, that's pretty far. What about Wasabi?
A: Wasabi? What kind of food do they serve?
M: Japanese food.

A: Hmm. How big is it?
M: It's pretty big.
A: Oh, I don't really like big restaurants. I know! What about Carlito's? My friend is the manager there.
M: Who is your friend?
A: Thomas. You know, Thomas.
M: Oh yeah. OK. Carlito's is good.

▶ **2.28** (Page 85)
1. chicken   2. seafood   3. fish
4. potatoes   5. lamb   6. rice   7. cheese
8. beef   9. pasta   10. chocolate

▶ **2.29** (Page 85)
W=Waiter A=Anna M=Mark
W: Hello. Do you have a reservation?
A: Yes. My name is Anna Pierce.
W: Ms. Pierce. A table for two?
A: That's right.
W: Come with me, please.
(later)
W: Are you ready to order?
M: Yes. I'd like the fish soup, please, and the lamb chops.
W: Certainly, sir. And for you ma'am?
A: I'd like the seafood cocktail, please, and the vegetable pasta.
W: Certainly. What would you like to drink?
M: Bottled water, please.
A: And can I get orange juice, please?
W: Certainly.
(later)
M: Oh, look at the time. It's pretty late.
A: Oh, my. It's 10:30.
M: Yes, it is. Excuse me. Can I have the check, please?
W: Of course.

UNIT 9 Your life

▶ **2.30** (Page 89)
First iPod in Stores: 2002
William and Kate – Royal Wedding: 2011
Tsunami in Southeast Asia: 2004
Titanic Disaster: 1912
Haiti Earthquake: 2010
Martin Luther King – I have a dream: 1963
Juan Peron: President of Argentina: 1946
Elvis Presley is dead: 1977

▶ **2.31** (Page 91)
I was an actor.
You were a singer.
He was happy.
She was born in 1982.
It was great.
We were singers.
They were rich.

▶ 2.32 (Page 92)

ML= Mei Ling I= Isabella K= Kenji

ML: OK. Your turn, Kenji.

K: Four! One, two, three, four. My first teacher!

I: OK, Kenji. Your first teacher. Forty-five seconds. Starting now!

K: OK, my first teacher was Mrs. Lloyd. She was about fifty years old.

ML: Was she a good teacher?

K: She was a good teacher, but I wasn't a good student.

I: Were you her favorite student?

K: I wasn't her favorite student. Koji was her favorite student.

ML: Was Koji your friend?

K: Yes, he . . . Oh no!

ML: Too bad, Kenji. OK, Isabella, your turn.

I: Two! One, two. Your last meal at a restaurant.

ML: OK, Isabella. Your last meal at a restaurant. Forty-five seconds. Starting now!

I: OK, my last meal at a restaurant was last week at Carluccio's.

K: Oh – that's great.

I: Yes, and . . . Oh no!

ML: Too bad, Isabella. OK, my turn. Five! One, two, three, four, five. My last vacation.

K: OK, Mei Ling Your last vacation. Forty-five seconds. Starting NOW!

ML: My last vacation was two years ago. It was to a Pacific island called Palau.

K: Were you with your parents?

ML: I wasn't with my parents. I was with my friend, Helen.

I: Was it a good vacation?

ML: It was a very good vacation. The hotel was very nice.

I: Were there any tourist attractions? Castles or palaces or . . .?

ML: There weren't any castles or palaces, but there were some beautiful beaches.

I: Was the weather nice?

ML: It was great. Sunny and hot . . .

K: Time's up! That's forty-five seconds. Good job, Mei Ling.

I: Yes, good job. Your turn again.

ML: Oh great! Six! One, two . . .

▶ 2.34 (Page 94)

4. do the laundry   2. clean the bathroom
1. vacuum the house   3. wash the dishes
6. cook dinner   5. iron a shirt

▶ 2.35 (Page 95)

AD=Aunt Dorothy J=Jeff B=Billy K=Karen F=Friend

1.

AD: Hello, Jeff. How are you?

J: Fine, thank you, Aunt Dorothy. How was your flight?

AD: Awful. Awful. There wasn't any coffee. There was no movie. And the flight was late. I'm so tired. Could you carry my suitcases? There are three.

J: Uh, yeah, sure.

2.

J: So, how was school, Billy?

B: Good!

J: Were you good for your teacher?

B: No! I was very bad! It was funny. Daddy, can I have ice cream for dinner?

J: No. Ice cream's not good for dinner.

3.

K: Hi, Jeff. I'm home.

J: Hello, darling. How was work?

K: It was OK. What's for dinner?

J: Spaghetti.

K: Oh. OK. Can I turn on the TV?

J: Uh, yeah, sure.

4.

F: So, Jeff. How was your week?

J: It wasn't very good. My Aunt Dorothy is here, my son is . . .

F: Oh! What's the matter? Jeff, could you pass the milk?

J: Yeah, sure.

▶ 2.37 (Page 97)

Louise: My school was called Washington High School. It was in San Francisco. I was there from 1981 to 1986. It was a good school, but I wasn't a very good student. I was good at sports and art, but I was pretty bad at math and science and languages. My favorite class was art. My teacher was Mr. Little, and he was great. My best friend was Katie Wilson. She was in my class and she was a lot of fun!

UNIT 10 Past and future events

▶ 2.38 (Page 99)

1. You lose your wallet.
2. A thief steals your cell phone.
3. You stay in bed all day.
4. You win the lottery.
5. You get married.
6. You find $10 on the street.
7. A police officer arrests you.
8. You move to a new house.
9. You break your leg.
10. You meet your favorite actor.

▶ 2.40 (Page 101)

wanted /ɪd/; worked /t/; asked /t/; talked /t/; moved /d/; closed /d/; started /ɪd/; cooked /t/; finished /t/; arrested /ɪd/; lived /d/; walked /t/; played /d/; listened /d/

▶ 2.41 (Page 101)

The story of the Mona Lisa (Part 2)

The Mona Lisa **moved** to Versailles, and then to the Louvre. In 1800, Napoleon **moved it** to his bedroom, but it **didn't stay** there. Four years later, it was back in the Louvre.

Then, on August 21st, 1911, the Louvre **closed** its doors. There was a big problem. The Mona Lisa wasn't there! Who was the thief? The police **talked to** lots of people. They **talked to** Picasso. Was he the thief? He wasn't. But they **didn't talk** to Vincenzo Peruggia.

▶ 2.43 (Page 103)

It's Christmas in July at Discount Electronics! Come down to Discount Electronics today. We've got low, low prices on hundreds of items.

A fantastic DVD player was a hundred and ninety-nine dollars. Sale price: one hundred and forty-nine.

A great laptop computer was thirteen thirty-nine. Sale price: one thousand and fifteen!

A beautiful Kenroko washing machine was six hundred and twenty-five dollars. Sale price: four hundred and sixty-five!

Hurry. Sale ends soon.

A great 32-inch flat screen TV was one thousand eighty-nine dollars Sale price: seven hundred and fifty.

A new fridge was five-oh-five. Sale price: four twenty-seven!

And a fantastic Bilman stove was four hundred and sixty-nine dollars. Sale price: three hundred and twenty-five!

Remember, our sale ends tomorrow, so hurry on down to Discount Electronics today!

▶ 2.44 (Page 104)

A=Abby C=Charlie N=Nick H=Haley

A: Hi, everyone. Sorry I'm late.

C: No problem. Nice to see you.

A: You, too Charlie. Hi Haley. You look great.

H: You, too.

A: Thanks. Hi Nick.

N: Nice to see you, Abby.

A: So how was your week, Nick?

N: Well, it was pretty interesting. I talked to my manager on Tuesday, and he gave me some news.

A: What?

N: My company is going to move to Texas.

H: To Texas! What are you going to do?

N: I'm not going to move to Texas. I'm going to find a new job.

C: Well, I'm glad you're going to stay here.

N: Yeah, me, too. You know, I was bored in that job, so it's OK really. How was your week, Abby?

A: Awful. Someone stole my cell phone.

H: That's terrible. Where? When?

A: Yesterday morning. On the train I think.

N: Too bad. So did you get a new phone?

A: No, I'm so busy, there wasn't time. I'm going to get a new phone tomorrow.

C: My week was busy, too. Lauren and I moved to a new apartment on Monday.

N: Oh great. How is it?

C: It's OK, but we're not going to stay there long. We're going to buy a house next year. How about you Haley?

H: Well, my week was very exciting. Daniel asked me to marry him.

A: He asked you to marry him! That's great!

N: What did you say?

H: I said yes!

C: Wow! Congratulations!

A: That's really exciting. When are you going to get married?

H: Oh, next year, I think, maybe in the summer. And of course you're all going to come to the wedding, . . .